I Am Brahman

ψ

A personal quest into the
Advaita Reality

First published by O Books, 2010
O Books is an imprint of John Hunt Publishing Ltd., The Bothy, Deershot Lodge, Park Lane, Ropley,
Hants, SO24 0BE, UK
office1@o-books.net
www.o-books.net

Distribution in:

UK and Europe
Orca Book Services Ltd
tradeorders@orcabookservices.co.uk
directorders@orcabookservices.co.uk
Tel: 01235 465521 Fax: 01235 465555
Int. code (44)

USA and Canada
NBN
custserv@nbnbooks.com
Tel: 1 800 462 6420 Fax: 1 800 338 4550

Australia and New Zealand
Brumby Books
sales@brumbybooks.com.au
Tel: 61 3 9761 5535 Fax: 61 3 9761 7095

Far East (offices in Singapore, Thailand,
Hong Kong, Taiwan)
Pansing Distribution Pte Ltd
kemal@pansing.com
Tel: 65 6319 9939 Fax: 65 6462 5761

South Africa
Stephan Phillips (pty) Ltd
Email: orders@stephanphillips.com
Tel: 27 21 4489839 Telefax: 27 21 4479879

Text copyright Maurice Anslow 2009

Design: Tom Davies

ISBN: 978 1 84694 366 9

A CIP catalogue record for this book is available
from the British Library.

Printed in the UK by CPI Antony Rowe, Chippenham, Wiltshire

I Am Brahman
ψ

A personal quest into the
Advaita Reality

Maurice Anslow

BOOKS

Winchester, UK
Washington, USA

ABOUT THE AUTHOR

Maurice Anslow has taken a life-long interest in comparative religion and mysticism. He obtained bachelor and master's degrees from London University in human evolution, prehistory and ancient history. After a career as a journalist he now practices as a transpersonal hypnotherapist. He has two sons and lives in Shropshire.

www.hypnotherapyforgrowth.co.uk

To
Mark and Paul

The Crossing Place

Down on the banks of the Ganges at Varanasi you enter into a different dimension of time and space. There really is nowhere like it. Here on these ghats is a world so raw, so surreal, that it borders on the frightening.

However did the Hindus create such a juncture of this world and the next? Here life throbs with a dizzying intensity. There is an urgency, a frantic disposition of the soul where the boundary between life and death seems to have been rubbed away.

Many Westerners will be shocked by this place. You can sense their discomfort, their sense of an alien spirituality. But linger. Expose yourself to this visceral scene and be tormented. Nowhere will ask such questions of your life – your actions, the karmic burden you carry with you. Go down to the Ganges at Varanasi and feel the very shock of being alive and the feeling that your life's account is in the reckoning.

The Hindus immerse themselves in the waters of the Ganges to wash away bad karma, to be cleansed by this mother goddess of waters and prepare themselves for their end. Here death is but part of life and the vainglory of this world means nothing. To die in Varanasi, which we used to call Benares, is a privilege with heaven within touching distance. You can feel it. These ghats seem to be stepping stones towards your destiny. It is like dicing with death before your time is up. If in any doubt, go to the burning ghats where you can witness corpses wrapped in their shrouds crackling in flames beside the river, which will bear away their souls. It is stomach churning and yet curiously beautiful. They fan the flames to make the mango logs burn brighter and afterwards boys will sieve the ashes for items of gold and jewellery.

Stashes of wood stand in stark testimony to the certainty of more corpses to come.

The West needs the East to remind it of the mystery and sanctity of life. In India, in particular, there is a determination to meet life head on, to confront it and live it intensely. Hindus do not seem overly worried about tomorrow. Nor are they particularly interested in the past. Hindus live in the present, the now, and live it as though every instant is their last. In any Indian city you see life being acted out with the most vivid sense of the now. In Benares this immediacy is even more apparent, with life in the narrow passageways behind the ghats taking place in a frenzy which draws its strength from the city's overpowering sense of spiritual urgency.

Varanasi is host to many religions. Hindu here rubs up against Muslim, Jain, Buddhist and Christian. But it is to the Hindu's Shiva that Varanasi really belongs.

The Hindus represent God in a trinity of forms – Brahma, the creator, Vishnu the preserver, and Shiva the destroyer. In Benares Shiva is pre-eminent, founder of the city and its protector. For Shiva, read God.

It is too easy to misunderstand the Hindu faith. Hinduism's multiplicities of gods makes no sense to the Western mind. Yet how much the West is missing through its spiritual narrow-mindedness.

Hinduism understands the alchemy of faith. God is not for us to understand, let alone see. We can only use our spiritual imagination to make an interior invocation of what lies beyond. This is the Hindu pantheon – a vast panoply of images to draw the seeker of truth towards a higher reality.

Religion can only be felt, not explained. Go into a Hindu temple and the god may seem a strange thing to worship – brightly coloured, garlanded with flowers and looking for all the world like a doll adorned. But pause a while and stare into the eyes of the god. Stare long and hard and be transported to somewhere beyond.

These gods of Hinduism represent magical visual formulas for spiritual insight and act like an intoxicant of the mind, shocking ourselves into understanding that we are spirit and part of the Divine. Because god is so multifacted, this entire Hindu pantheon has developed to represent all aspects of the human reality. There are gods like Ganesha to represent luck, Krishna to reflect pleasure, Rama for righteousness, Lakshmi for fortune and beauty, Durga for realisation, Sarasvati for wisdom and speech, and so on.

Hinduism is a religion that seeks to see God reflected in everything because it knows that there is only one reality, the all-pervading oneness of the universe, the one Brahman presence that not only pervades everything but *is* everything. To describe Hinduism as polytheistic is a mistake born of a Judeo-Christian perspective. Hindus also worship one God but they call it by many different names and see it from different angles in its many different guises.

When a Hindu does puja to one of the many incarnations of Vishnu, he or she is worshipping God just as much as a Christian, a Muslim or a Jew. It is a shame that religions view each other as wrong when they all really seek the same thing. The religions have much to learn from each other. Hinduism's everlasting gift to mankind has been its openness to other faiths and its refusal to be dogmatic or creed-based.

In India Christians and Hindus regularly celebrate each other's festivals. Rickshaw drivers have pictures of Jesus in their cabs alongside images of their favourite Hindu gods. "Jesus is my friend," one Hindu said to me.

Underlying this openness and magnanimity towards all faiths is the deep metaphysical roots of the Hindu faith which represent the most profound philosophical enquiry man has yet made into the nature of reality. Enshrined in the ancient Vedas and developed most expressively in the Upanishads, the metaphysical insight of the Vedanta tradition lends Hinduism a substructure, which does not exist in other faiths.

It is to the ancient wisdom of India that many scientists are now turning to understand the fundamental workings of the cosmos.

Here on the banks of the Ganges the philosophical roots of their faith may seem a long way from the devotion of these Hindus. Here the bathers at the ghats are absorbed in their swimming, splashing, cupping the waters in their hands, washing themselves and drying out their clothes. They sit mostly in male-only or female-only groups, setting up makeshift shrines at the top of the steps and talking to the learned Brahmins. This is where they want to be, the ultimate destination for pilgrimage and to front up their own personal realities in a way that is both humble and daring at the same time.

There is a golden light over the ghats that gives the place a strange ethereal glow, otherworldly and slightly disturbing. Don't believe the photographs or films you see of Varanasi. They give the place a romantic, picturesque gloss. The reality is different. The ghats and surrounds at Varanasi, this meeting place of two worlds, are dirty and smelly. Bulls, dogs and goats wander as freely here as they do anywhere in India. Hawkers are everywhere and you are just as likely to receive an ayurvedic massage, a boat trip or an offer to buy silks as you are to have a spiritual experience. A combination of the smell and the sheer rawness of its thronging humanity can make you very quickly feel sick to the stomach. It is a throbbing daunting place with a hint of menace in the air.

Often the high-pitched feelings in Benares boil over into riots, shootings and the occasional terrorist incident. The police sometimes make a show of force before a religious festival because the rule of law needs occasionally to re-assert itself here. All of India's zest and passion for life seems to have been brought to fever pitch in Varanasi.

Imagine distilling life into its essential raw reality and taking it to the edge of a cliff and that is the holy city of Varanasi. In the sepulchral city of Varanasi the people seem to have taken on a different form and you encounter wandering figures along the ghats that appear like ghosts, neither in one world or another. The veil is thin in Varanasi.

I am at one of the burnings ghats, viewing the cremations from a boat on the river. Two feet can be clearly seen sticking out of the conflagration. The corpse's blackened arms are projecting in the air, rigor-mortis fashion. One of the low-caste Hindus who attend these pyres comes with a stick and bends a leg backwards, snapping it into the flames. Life and death come face to face besides the Ganges at Varanasi.

ψ

This small book is a personal reach into Vedantic Hinduism and an attempt to describe to a Western reader the truth, and the feeling of that truth, which has been gleaned over the millennia by the fully realised souls that have graced India. This is more a personal spiritual journey than a monologue on Indian philosophy and it must bear all its faults and limitations for that. Can a Westerner ever really expect to understand the Eastern mind-set? Possibly not, but there is now a growing sway of sympathy in the West towards the wisdom of the East and this author counts himself amongst those who are drawn towards an embrace of the Vedantic tradition.

I started this particular personal journey in Glastonbury, England's most famous pilgrimage centre and where so many spiritual currents seem to come together. I was in retreat at a nearby monastic centre when I realised that even the most traditional Christian monks were reaching out for a broader spiritual understanding.

One night after dinner an elderly monk came up to me with great excitement to tell me he had just read Eckhart Tolle's ground-breaking New Age masterpiece The Power of Now, and had rarely seen such a brilliant interpretation of the words of Christ. The first thing I did when I left the monastery was to go back to Glastonbury and buy Eckhart Tolle's book. Shortly, I would leave for India but by then I would have read what the monk had been so eager for me to see.

Do not underestimate how shocking it will be to travel towards Brahman. T.S. Elliot once said that man couldn't take too much reality. We baulk at too much truth like we blind ourselves to the likelihood of our own death. How much easier to live in a fug of material comforts. Even in India the popular face of Hinduism can be seen way below the high philosophical flight of the non-dual Advaita reality.

In religion, however, it pays to start somewhere, anywhere. As the Buddhists say; there are many paths to God and one should not sit on the fence too long trying to choose one.

Varanasi is the best place to start this quest for Brahman realisation. This is the spiritual hub of India. One is not surprised that the Buddha, who was according to Hinduism the seventh and last incarnation of Vishnu, preached his first sermon a few miles from Varanasi at Sarnath. There seems little question that spirituality condenses in certain physical locations. Places made holy through prayer. Places, which contain a huge build-up of positive karma that seems to hover in the air to be grasped by those seeking truth. We ourselves create these places that in India they call "tirthas" – crossing places between temporal and spiritual realities. Varanasi has this sense of a crossing place like nowhere else on Earth. Why is that?

The ghats at Varanasi face directly East into the rising sun. Descending the steps (ghats) down to the river is like approaching some deeper reality. It is as though the city is built on a fault line of consciousness where piety over the ages has created a shock zone to remind us not only of our mortality but also of what constitutes our essential selves.

We are Brahman, the single unitary ground consciousness of

the universe which is God. All else, as the Hindus know, is passing and essentially illusory. In Varanasi the self can melt away and what you think of as "you" no longer stands and you can try to merge into that infinite swathe of consciousness that is Brahman. Immersion of the body into the Ganges is a metaphor for this absorption into the One, the ridding of karma through its washing in the overwhelming sea of cosmic consciousness.

Big rivers like the Ganges have this spiritual pull on man. Their enduring characteristic lends rivers that mother or basing feeling which man responds to by regarding the waters as sacred. That is what the realisation of Brahman requires – the intuition that you are part of a greater whole and that your very consciousness is not a product of brain-centred mind but is part of the unitive awareness of God.

They say that Varanasi is outside of time. It certainly feels like that for Varanasi gives the impression that time is suspended at the place where Brahman is breaking through.

For the Hindus Varanasi is the place to come and die because they believe souls will achieve final liberation from the cycle of death and rebirth just by virtue of being within the holy city when you breath your last. It is raw – but shouldn't ultimate reality have a feeling of rawness about it? We live our lives through a glass darkly doing anything but face the reality of which we are a part. The Brahman within us, which the Hindus call the atman, is trapped and limited by our bodies and minds. The atman soul reality of each one of us is here to experience, learn, work out its karma and ultimately to realise itself and thus add to the self-realisation of the one-God consciousness.

The single quality of the universe is consciousness, self-awareness, and the wonder is that this reflection grows and enhances itself through incarnation in material suffering forms. God is learning, growing, never still through its extended awareness in all conscious forms. The highest form of atman awareness is when it knows it is Brahman and God's consciousness becomes that much wider and more complete. Ultimately, we are the process of God knowing itself.

Immersion of the body in the Ganges is a physical expression of the spiritual yearning for oneness with Brahman. The atman is reabsorbed into Brahman. Brahman makes our earthly imperfections – call them sins if you like – seem small and trivial. A sin is no more than that which blocks our souls from seeing their Brahman reality. A sin is ourselves being slaved to selfish material satisfaction and as such occludes our ability to see our soul identity.

For us humans, evolved from an animal process, we are predetermined to fail in our attempts to understand our higher reality. In Christianity they call it original sin. But that is the whole point of it. It is difficult and it is meant to be difficult. We need help and that is why religion has evolved to create mechanisms by which we can obvert our animal incarnation and identity ourselves with our God consciousness. That is why Christ became incarnate on Earth, to act as a shepherd for our souls so that our imperfections could be passed over, and through faith – sheer faith – we were guaranteed a passage through endless capture in flesh.

Shiva is represented in various forms but in Benares it is most common to see him as the lingum, apparently a phallic symbol which is actually a curious mixture of male and female characteristics. How can you worship a small, rounded column of stone? Visit one of these linga temples and watch the faithful attend their puja before the flower-adorned column, the temple bells being rung, incense swirling around the shrine, and open yourself to the strange intoxication that Hinduism has learned to conjure. To peer into the beyond you need to put on different eyes and see through the temporal to the reality of Brahman.

Because our minds act to close down our soul reality and limit the extent of our understanding, you have to be nudged into a new state by the contemplation of strange imagery, striking sounds and smells. At the heart of Hinduism is this age-old ability to incant the religious experience through imagery and sound –the more idiosyncratic and strange the better.

Ah, you may say, but surely Shiva does not really exist? As soon as you ask that you have lost the point. Shiva does exist because Hindus have created him as a spiritual reality, an inner reflection of man-centred consciousness projected onto the universal screen of Brahman. To say that the spiritual is not real is to have missed the big picture. The Vedic tradition is that consciousness creates reality and what we see as real is a kind of consensus view of the material world, which is always changing, temporal, and in flux. So the religious imagination is part of Brahman consciousness and to bear witness to Shiva is as real as seeing a rock, a tree or anything.

To try and explain this Brahman reality, and how it must inform us of not only our true identity but of the power latent within us, is the purpose of this book. I will not dwell over-long over the theology of Hinduism because that has been done on many occasions. Rather, I seek in all humility to take the reader on a spiritual journey to see if we can "feel out" the reality of Brahman and make it as visceral as the emotional experience down beside the Ganges at Varanasi.

ψ   ˎ

Into The Advaita Reality

It is Christmas Eve in Chennai and I am caught between my own tradition of midnight mass and the urge to explore a different spirituality. I decide on an evening visit to the oldest temple structure in the city, the Parthasarathi Temple dating from the eighth century and dedicated to Krishna as the royal charioteer. The god is being paraded inside the temple in an ear-splitting tempest of drum beating and chanting which is otherworldly and even a little alarming. That is what these Hindu ceremonies do – shock the observer into a changed mindset. The blaze of colour and sound that accompanies worship of the god, acts to make our usual jumble of mind-centred consciousness move over for a moment and permit our inner soul-based awareness to shine through. All very different from the hushed worship of Christian church services at this time of year. The worst thing you can do, however, is to judge the practices of one religion from the standpoint of another tradition.

We must be *feeling* individuals, hungry for inner experience and humble in our attempts to explore other peoples' spirituality. True, Hinduism can seem impenetrable from a Western mind-set. Hindus are completely unabashed about how money and their gods seem to go together so easily. In this temple there are stalls piled with cheap religious items for sale, even in the inner sanctum and outside in the forecourt prepare to be assailed by hordes of women trying to relieve you of your cash as you leave. The trick is to be swamped in the very now-ness of Hindu spirituality. In this tradition there is no separation between God and Mammon or between God and anything. All is one and immediate, the moment is perfect in its completeness. God is not distant, somehow separate from our life, but right down here and dirty, in a temple that fits seamlessly into the rest of Indian life.

I move on to St George's church for a midnight service and the touching loveliness of Indian Christianity. The classical style church is lit up like a Christmas tree and hundreds of worshippers are seated in rows outside the packed church. The men are nearly all in suits and the women are wearing their finest saris. They take their religion seriously in India so don't come to the conclusion that Christianity is on the wane until you have seen how vivid the faith still is in its Eastern manifestation.

The sense of Christ's presence is very tangible on Christmas Eve and these Indian faithful sit patiently during a very long service, waiting to acknowledge that God has become manifest for all.

You can perhaps sense that same kind of exclusivity and sense of being superior that unfortunately so lets down most Christian congregations, but perhaps that comes naturally with religious conviction. What matters is what is going on inside you, and who is to know the individual spiritualities of these worshippers?

If you sense the nearness of Christ it is because you have consciously willed his presence in the oneness of Brahman space. Christ is always there and you only have to ask and there becomes no distinction between your consciousness and his.

Indian Christians do not talk about Brahman but they could do. The Holy Spirit of the Christians is just another way of saying Brahman, except that Christians do not understand the Indian concept of non-duality or Advaita. Christians see God as separate and somehow "up there". Even though Christ lived an Earthly life, Christ too is seen as separate and sits at God's right hand, while the Holy Spirit is the carrier of grace from the Godhead to us. If Christians could get away from making these distinctions or dualities then not only would their faith be strengthened but it would make more sense too. Christ is not separate from God but an incarnation of God's consciousness. The Holy Spirit is the ground consciousness of the universe, God's awareness onto which everything else is painted.

Chennai has good pedigree in the search for the Advaita Reality because this is the home of the Theosophical Society that was founded in 1875 to advocate the oneness of world religions and to promote an open-minded approach to exploring all spiritualities. The Theosophical Society has been one of the major routes by which Eastern philosophy has been brought to the West and it still remains at the forefront of spiritual and metaphysical enquiry. No one religion or philosophy dominates the Theosophical Society, but it would be true to say that the Indian concept of Oneness permeates most of its discussions and writings.

I have come to the annual week-long meeting of the Theosophical Society, which is held just after Christmas at its spacious headquarters in the Adyar district of south Chennai. It is reassuring how ordinary everyone is and how, rather than pack the day with talks, most of the time is left free to wander the beautiful gardens and have time to meditate or think. Normally, I shy away from joining things and distrust group activities but there is nothing to offend here. By definition the Theosophical Society is non-denominational and dedicated to the search rather than claiming to have the answer, so there are no cults or fundamentalists, no fanatics or dogmatics. Most of the delegates seem to be of Hindu background which is encouraging because it is further evidence of how this tradition constantly produces deep thinkers and an exploratory as opposed to a prosaic approach to religion.

What a hotbed of spirituality India has to offer! Little wonder that this country has often been seen as the font of all religion. All the branches of world faith have drawn sustenance from the soil of India. One thinks especially of how Islam flourished in India under the sultans and mughals, but also developed a distinctive flavour of its own and actually found an accommodation with the native Hinduism. India was where Buddhism, Jainism and Sikhism sprouted from the ages old Vedic roots of

Hinduism. Christianity has also found fertile ground and a faithful following in India, as I saw beneath the twinkling Christmas lights of the church in Chennai.

Despite the obvious importance of Hinduism in the history of religious enquiry, it remains that the faith has been poorly understood in the West, where for a long time it suffered under the "superiority" of Christianity. This was a great shame because the philosophical roots of Hinduism represent the oldest known religious thinking and its metaphysical insight has no parallel in any other tradition.

Only in the Gospel of John and St. Paul's First Letter to the Romans does the Christian New Testament get close to the profound speculations about reality that have come out of India. In the 20th century, interest started to emerge in the West in the deep thinking underlying Hinduism, and this sympathy with Eastern philosophy underpins much of New Age religious thought in the West. At its best the New Age revival which has been growing since the 1960s, is promising to build a bridge between East and West and to redraft the Vedic tradition into something that makes sense to the modern mind.

Today's Western approach to Hinduism sees two important elements of thinking. The first is known as Vedanta and simply means "the end of the Vedas". The corpus of the Vedanta was the summing up of what was in the original Vedas. The other element is the concept of Advaita that grows out of Vedanta to form the single most important contribution that India has made to world philosophy. Vedanta and Advaita comprise the foundation of the Hindu tradition but they are, in fact, an interpretation of existence that can easily stand outside any one religious practice while absorbing them all at the same time. It is perfectly possible to regard oneself as a Vedantin or an Advaitin without prescribing to Hindu religious practice. The wisdom of the Vedic tradition stands alone which is why it has started to draw so much attention from people of other faiths or those of no particular faith at all.

One of the most compelling aspects of the Hindu tradition is its sheer antiquity. There was no "revelation" moment we can trace nor any one inspired individual who can be located in historical time to say where it all began. The fact that a statuette of a seated Shiva in a yoga position was discovered amongst the ruins of the Indus Valley civilisation at Mohenjo-daro and dated to 3250 BC indicates that we are dealing with a religion whose roots are deep in prehistoric time. We should not underestimate how sophisticated religious thinking in the world was at this time. This was the era when the first pyramids were being erected in Egypt and mysterious Stonehenge had its origins in stone age England. There is no reason at all why the nature of reality could not be gleaned by someone in meditation more than 5,000 years ago.

Ideas were being transmitted between cultures often far apart and religious insight may have been so vivid in those days that many societies were effectively in the thrall of priests and shamans. Neolithic society was giving way to settled groups and the first cities where differentiation of labour would allow some to pursue religious and philosophical enquiry.

We do not know how far the native religion had developed by the time Aryan peoples from the northwest arrived on the Indian sub-continent around 2000 BC. These Aryans, however, seem to have been responsible for bringing not only a more formal approach to Indian religion but also a deep philosophical and metaphysical foundation to which the native faith could adhere.

The Aryans had their own gods and their religion was based on ritual sacrifice conducted with hymns sung in an ancient form of Sanskrit. These hymns date to around 1500-1000 BC. Sometime later commentaries were added to these hymns to become the Vedas. These commentaries were written by the priests, whose class we call Brahmins, whose job was to ensure the ancient rites were preserved for continuity and who, to this day, are the class who maintain India's philosophic and ritual traditions. It is at this point in human history that the remarkable insight into reality arrived, which the whole world is now blessed with. Hinduism is the heir of this tradition. Somewhere, at this time in prehistoric dusty India, the souls of the poets soared and touched an inspired vision of man's place in the universe and intuited his true identity.

The term Veda means literally "to know" and the four ancient texts represent that point at which poetic religious inspiration was formalised into ritual instruction. In the Vedas we see the primordial religious response where natural forces are invested with supernatural deities; so that we have gods who represent nature elements, like Agni (fire) and Parjanya (rain). But we also see the beginnings of mankind's conviction that it can make a relationship with these higher realities, with the introduction of human forms like Indra (warrior), Rudra (storms, later to emerge as Shiva) and Vishnu.

Then the Vedas soar into metaphysical speculation and we first come into contact with the concept of Brahman, that almost untranslatable Sanskrit word which means the God presence behind everything, the ground consciousness of the universe.

This is the moment that mankind, evolved over the millennia with all the host of Earth's animal life, stands in awe of consciousness itself:

"By Brahman was this earth established;
Brahman the heavens fixed on high;
Brahman this atmosphere, this wide expanse,
Established above, athwart."

Atharva-Veda 25

The major statement of the Brahman concept came with the writing of the Upanishads that developed out of the Vedas themselves and were completed by 500 BC. There are between

100 and 200 Upanishad texts, depending on what source you use, but today we tend to look at just ten of them.

The ninth century philosopher and mystic Shankara selected these ten Upanishads for special commentary at a time when Hindus needed reminding about the mystical core at the centre of their religion. Shankara was responsible for developing the Advaita branch of Vedanta that can be looked upon as the purist extrapolation of meaning from the Upanishads themselves. The Upanishads are the definitive and unequivocal exposition of the belief that Brahman is the nature of reality and our own true identity. All is Brahman, all is in a unitive state with God, and the appearance of a duality between spirit and matter is an illusion. Brahman is the projection of God's consciousness throughout time and space – indeed, Brahman is time and space.

Brahman is a Sanskrit word for which there is no equivalent in any other language. The word is a noun but not a noun, for the pundits tell us that Brahman cannot be particularised, is formless and characterless and beyond description. The word Brahman represents more of an intuitive feeling, an adjective for something sensed, than a naming of something "out there". Brahman is a word of total inclusiveness that tries to convey the sense that everything is embraced within a universal ground awareness and that this is the only enduring reality.

Brahman is the Holy Spirit of Christian description by another name. Pure spirit is pure consciousness, the one God awareness untainted by incarnation into material forms. When St John's Gospel begins,

"In the beginning was the Word,

And the Word was with God, And the Word was God,"

just exchange "Word" for "Brahman" and we are talking about the same thing.

Brahman is God's consciousness at large – the all-pervading mirror of awareness upon which the dance of the material universe takes place. Brahman is not distinct from God but a projection of God. In the Hindu tradition when we think of this God at the centre of Brahman it is called Isvara and can be seen as the personal aspect of the Godhead. But there is no need to build distinctions between Brahman and God because they are One – awareness and energy at the same time.

In the beginning was Awareness, and the Awareness was with God, and God was the Awareness. With apologies to St John's Gospel this is perhaps another way of trying to describe that this ground awareness is the fundamental nature of Reality. Awareness is because no other state is possible. The Godhead is the gathering together of this Awareness into creative and evolutionary energy which is Brahman and turning it into consciousness by a superposition of material forms.

To have consciousness there must be a subject to be conscious of while awareness need be nothing than just aware. When the awareness becomes aware of itself then God emerges, the personal Isvara at the centre of itself.

Jesus said that, "Before Abraham was I am." Was he not saying that before this world existed there was just awareness aware of itself? It is through the tipping point of the God-moment, that Isvara point, that Awareness becomes Brahman with the creative energy to evolve a sentient universe. The universe we see is not other than God, but God as Brahman where awareness becomes consciousness.

"The deathless Self meditated upon
Himself and projected the universe
As evolutionary energy"

Mundaka Upanishad

While we associate Brahman with the Hindu faith it is quite easy to see reference to this same concept of an underlying super-reality in all religions. In fact, the *essence* of all religious beliefs all point in the same direction and this is most clearly seen when you look at the mystical traditions of each faith.

Buddhism, which has grown out of Hinduism, is quite familiar with a universal awareness. The Tibetan Book of the Dead gives great space to discussing the nature of awareness and the distinction between what we call mind and the "intrinsic mind".

"Within this intrinsic awareness,
Which penetrates ordinary consciousness to the core,
There is no duality between the object of meditation
and the meditator."

The Tibetan Book of the Dead

Islam, too, likes to talk about the "Absolute" and identifies it with original consciousness. Consider how the Sufi mystic Hazrat Inayat Khan puts it:

"A consciousness arose out of this Absolute, a consciousness of existence. There was nothing of which the Absolute could be conscious – only of its existence...... Out of this consciousness of existence a sense developed, the sense: I exist."

Inayat Khan in The Soul – Whence and Wither

In the book of ancient Chinese wisdom called the Tao Te Ching we again see the concept of a universal underlying consciousness that is called the Tao:

"Eyes look but cannot see it
Ears listen but cannot hear it
Hands grasp but cannot touch it
Beyond the senses lies the great Unity-
Invisible, inaudible, intangible"

Tao Te Ching, Verse 14

In Christianity we have alluded to the opening words of John's Gospel but the Christian mystical tradition is littered with examples where the faith sounds as though its metaphysical basis is hardly any different to Hinduism. The medieval English mystic Julian of Norwich had a series of contemplative experiences which all tended towards this experience of Oneness that would not have been out of place in the Upanishads.

> "It is a great thing to know in our heart that God, our Maker, indwells our soul.
> Even greater is it to know that our soul, our created soul, dwells in the substance of God. Of that substance, God, are what we are!"
>
> *Julian of Norwich, Revelation of Divine Love*

Another medieval Christian mystic and priest whose writings and sermons have strong parallels with Hindu philosophy is Meister Eckhart who, just like his fellow Indian theologians, knew that the soul's oneness with God could be experienced now:

> "There is One in which the entire multitude participates, through which the multitude is one and is whole, and this One is God. Moreover the multitude is in it alone.
> Therefore all things are the One by means of the One alone"
>
> *Meister Eckhart, A Sermon, translated by Robert Forman*

The awareness that our souls are our true reality and that they are part of God's universal soul resonates throughout all faiths. In the Hindu faith they say that our individual souls, described as the "atman", are at all times part of Brahman. The soul is always immersed in Brahman and never separate from it. But the soul is individuated in Brahman and its trial through incarnation in material flesh is part of the dynamic process whereby Brahman consciousness is continually enriched and heightened.

It is too much to imagine that God would spend eternity just contemplating itself. Only through Brahman's inhabitation of material form does God fully experience itself and grow. God is never static but is all the time experiencing the full material universe in every detail. We are part of God's awareness and never separate from God's experience of itself. This is not the same as the monist view that we *are* God. In Hinduism, we are a projection of God but not God itself. Just as a photon of light emitted from the sun is from the sun but you cannot say that it *is* the sun, so atman consciousness is of God, or from God, but not God itself. Brahman is the universal projection of God's consciousness like a great multi-dimensional mirror onto which all sense and mind experience is reflected.

Brahman is the consciousness of the universe without which awareness cannot exist. When we meditate the object is to turn off our sense of self and let the one Brahman consciousness absorb the atman soul back into itself. To experience this oneness is to experience bliss, total oneness with Brahman and thus the consciousness of God.

What does Brahman feel like? The pundits tell us that Brahman is indescribable because we have no words that can account for the perfection of pure BEING. To achieve oneness with Brahman is to know BEING and it is to see reality from the perspective of God.

Some great souls have achieved this realisation. They have exchanged a singular identity for the greater identity but even they must resort to parables and metaphor to put that condition into human terms. We can, however, attempt a description of what it feels like *to approach* Brahman. There is only one word we have in our vocabulary which can express the real quality of Brahman and that is love. The sensation which meditation provides when you are beginning to glimpse Brahman can only be described as like being totally in love.

This is, of course, saying no more than all the religions have told us through all time. The importance of love as the ultimate expression of God and our responses to God is axiomatic to all faiths. But why is this? Why should love be so important when the universe is clearly full of so much destruction, hate, fear and violence?

Love is a word we use to express a feeling we experience in our earthly lives. We know this feeling at its sweetest when we fall in love with our partner or our child, and it is the most overwhelming and dazzling of all our mortal feelings. Examine love a little closer, however, and it is not hard to see why it has to be the feeling or quality we experience of Brahman becoming closer. To be in love is to experience complete oneness with another person. This sense of oneness can be so extreme that you feel your loved one and yourself have become one person. It is the same with Brahman consciousness. Brahman is one. Brahman is the projection of the one-god consciousness and in its grasp everything is one with everything else. The oneness we feel in miniature when we love someone is the nature of Brahman itself, which holds everything as one in a great cosmic bond of love. Love is the ultimate oneness and Brahman feels like that because it is oneness.

"The Lord of love is one".
Shurtashvantara Upanishad 2

Maybe it would be better if we had a different word for love? Many people find it difficult to equate a God of love with a creation that contains so much suffering. But this is because we fail to see what love means in its cosmic sense. God's love is not some sentimental, slushy thing in which everything is lovely. God's love is projected as the oneness of its Brahman consciousness, in the fact that it holds everything within its net and that all is part of itself. God's love is oneness but it feels the same as we experience when we fall in love in this mortal realm.

ψ

The term Advaita simply means "non-dual" and it can be regarded as perhaps the central, but not only, form of Vedanta. Advaita Vedanta was Shankara's great gift to Hindu religious thinking and it has been the most enduring argument about the nature of reality ever to come out of India. To Shankara there was no reality other than Brahman and the world of forms we experience is a function of Brahman, a temporary and passing world that ceases to exist once we have found perfect unity with Brahman. To grasp this central point about the unitary, non-dual nature of reality as explained by Advaita, is absolutely essential for the questing spirit. But it is a very difficult concept and requires for its full realisation not so much mental agility as the fruits of deep meditation.

Shankara's great problem was to explain that if everything is formless Brahman how did the material world come about? Advaita says that the phenomenal world we experience is Maya – a superimposition on the surface of Brahman and it is only real because we see it in ignorance of Brahman. This is not the same as saying that the world is an illusion. The world is real enough but it is not the Absolute Reality and it drops away completely when we are in full knowledge and experience of Brahman.

The concept of Maya is the most difficult to understand in Advaita philosophy and it is not to say that even Shankara explained it satisfactorily. Be it enough for us ordinary enquirers to accept that the act of creation, of God through its Brahman consciousness projecting a material "surface" on the Absolute, that a distortion of Reality takes place and that any sense perception within that distortion is blinded from seeing the Absolute Reality beneath. Only through the super-consciousness of deep meditation can we reach beyond our world of Maya and witness Brahman.

Another way of approaching this problem of Maya is to

consider that we only see (or hear, or feel, or think) what we want to see or hear, or feel, or think, or perhaps more accurately, we only see what we have been conditioned to see. Consider that this material Maya world in which we live, is infinitely plastic and has no absolute reality other than the way it is "fixed" by being consciously observed.

Science tells us that at the fundamental quantum level everything is in a state of uncertainty with no fixable reality other than that as determined by the observer. Shankara would no doubt agree but he was seeing the implications of this on a universal scale and of how there could only ever be the one Brahman (God consciousness) level of Absolute Reality.

Perhaps the best "proof" of the unreality of the material world as opposed to the Absolute nature of Brahman is the performance of miracles by generations of saints, holy men, avatars and swamis. A miracle changes reality. One physical form is changed into another or a physical form is created from nothing. To change water into wine, cure the sick, appear in two places at once or produce objects out of the air defies the laws of science but these miracles are possible when a soul has achieved super-consciousness, knows that it is Brahman and has the power to produce its own Maya effects. Miracles come from knowledge of Brahman and how that Brahman consciousness is the creative power (or "spirit" if you like) of God. To perform a miracle the enlightened soul is drawing down the power of Brahman to change one Maya illusion into another.

Christ called this power the Holy Spirit but that is Brahman by another name. The important thing to understand is that Brahman is actually a creative power, the vehicle through which the will of God acts. To realise that you are part of Brahman, that your consciousness, your true identity, is Brahman means that you are at one with the creative force of the universe and your will can access that force to act, to some degree, as it wishes.

"Not only is the entire universe reflected in man, but also the power to control the universe is waiting to be used by him."

In "I Am That – Talks with Sri Nisargadatta Maharaj"

Miracles are not *per se* the necessary result of Brahman awareness. Jesus told his disciples to keep quiet about his miracle working. The 19th century Indian mystic Ramakrishna instructed his followers to avoid dabbling in miracles. But true knowledge of Brahman permits the knower to see into the nature of Maya and to understand that the material world has no Absolute existence and that it is simply a superimposition on Brahman, a thought or dream of the underlying consciousness of the universe. This is the hardest leap to make and mere words can never explain the full meaning of the Brahman Reality. Usually, only in meditation can we ever hope to experience Brahman and when we do the Maya world disappears and its very insubstantial nature becomes clear. Only in meditation can we achieve that state of super-consciousness when we witness that our personal conscious identity is not our mind or body existing in a material world but the one consciousness of Brahman that alone allows what we call reality to exist.

To do that we have to rid ourselves of the conventional mind-set that sees us as observers of a reality in which we are set. There is no other reality than that of God's consciousness that we call Brahman. That consciousness, the Self-Awareness of the universe, determines everything that exists and because you are an inseparable part of that same Brahman then you too are determining what exists.

Miracles are performed when the Atman has merged back into Brahman, when we have lost our identity with our material form and when nothing is left but the creative willpower that is pure consciousness. This link between will and consciousness is important. In Vedanta it is common to hear that Brahman is formless and has no qualities. But Brahman is the vehicle through which God's will is enacted, through which the creation occurs. Thus Brahman is an agent or power and not just a passive reflector of all conscious experience. The consciousness of Brahman has potency; an active force which when conjured by individual willpower is the creative and evolutionary force in the universe. God, the Isvara at the centre of all Brahman, we can imagine as permanently acting through Brahman and experiencing at all times the totality of all consciousness. But in small though not insignificant ways, we as knowers of Brahman can also summon its creative power and that is how enlightened souls have been able to perform the miracles that have been borne witness to over the ages. Sadhus and Yogis often attain these powers and relinquish them again in acknowledgment that they are not enlightenment. This is not to say that we *should* want to be miracle-makers and there are many reasons why it is perhaps not necessary for us to go there. There must have been many more individuals who became aware of the potential to be miracle-makers than ever decided to act upon their knowledge. The reason miracles are important, however, is that they provide the certainty that someone has real knowledge of the higher reality and that what they say or write is worth our attention.

ψ

One of the most striking features about modern Hinduism is the way it seems almost divorced from its Vedic origins. To witness temple worship of Shiva and Vishnu and their many incarnations it is not at all obvious that there is any reference, either in spirituality or ritual practice, to Vedanta or even the Upanishads. In Chennai, when I witnessed the veneration of Krishna at the Parthasarathi Temple, the words of the Upanishads seemed a long way away. Some observers of Hinduism have concluded that there are, in fact, two strands to the Hindu tradition; one the abstract philosophy of the Vedas/Vedanta, the other the populist attachment to temple ritual and celebration of a personalised god with whom the worshipper has an intimate bond. Krishna, for example, is seen as a god with very human characteristics and inclinations. But this is the same Krishna who appears in the Bhagavad Gita to instruct the warrior Arjuna in the deepest meaning of life and whose words ring with the same wisdom that you will find in the Upanishads.

"The joy supreme comes to the Yogi whose heart is still, whose passions are peace, who is pure from sin, who is one with Brahman, with God."

Bhagavad Gita

Just because most worshippers need to put a face, an icon or an image to represent the Divine does not mean they don't see it as God. It is the depth of awareness created through using the religious imagination that matters. Krishna is an evocation of God; a vision of an aspect of the divine nature and Krishna exists within Brahman because nothing can exist outside of the One. The Hindu gods are like contact points within Brahman, spiritual nodes where the many becomes focused onto the One.

Both the philosophical and ritual strands of Hinduism ultimately come together in their agreement that humankind's object is to achieve liberation from the cycle of birth and death through ultimate realisation of his God nature. This process in Hinduism is known as moksha and it the same as the Buddhist concept of nirvana. From the cleverest philosopher to the most humble temple worshipper everyone agrees that the path is to abandon our sense of ourselves and seek unity with God.

"As long as we think we are the ego
We feel attached and fall into sorrow,
But realize we are the Self, the Lord
Of Life, and you will be freed from sorrow.

27

When you realise that you are the Self,
Supreme source of light, supreme source of love,
You transcend the duality of life
And enter into the unitive state."

Mundaka Upanishad

The path along which we travel to achieve this goal of spiritual release is known as dharma and these paths are many because what suits one individual is not necessarily what someone else requires. Dharma is our true personal duty and the essence of our individual lives. For Arjuna in the Gita, his dharma was to do battle against the unrighteous.

Do you know what your own dharma is? Have you ever felt there was an undercurrent to your life, a theme, a sense of something you feel you must do? It could be as simple as to help others or to raise a family, as straightforward as to do your job to the best of your ability, or to do research . Sometimes this dharma may be a challenge and you feel that you want to struggle against it. Arjuna had to be persuaded by Krishna that his course was the right one, just as we all wonder whether the course we are on is worth it or the right one.

Our individual dharmas are prescribed for us because it is the way in which we will work out or address the karma of our past (see chapter five) which is the collected consequences of acts we have undertaken in this and previous lives.

Krishna says in the Gita that karma "is the force of creation, wherefrom all things have their life." In other words karma is the force of action, the actual experiential aspect of Brahman that includes all our individual lives.

The test of whether our dharma is the correct one is to ask at all times whether it leads us towards the divine, regardless of how far we actually climb towards our own moksha. All tasks we perform should be done selflessly and in the spirit of giving. With selfless duty comes a predisposition to seek reference to

God in our lives; any dharma will ultimately be fruitless unless it leads to spiritual devotion. Those Hindus in their temple in Chennai know that by worshipping Krishna they are setting their sights on God, and that Krishna, no less than a Christ or any other God image, is the portal through which they will reach true knowledge.

"For those who take refuge in me and strive to be free from age and death, they know Brahman, they know Atman, and they know what Karma is."

Bhagavad Gita

Followers of Krishna will not need any reminding that it is the act of devotion which is central to obtaining knowledge of Brahman and achieving progress on the path to moksha. We live in an age where spiritual devotion has been on the wane and where even believers in God see no need for regular devotions. This is a great mistake because you cannot set the mind towards God without the practice of devotion. In the Bhagavad Gita the essentials of devotion were called yoga and it was this that Krishna explained to Arjuna. Faced with imminent battle Arjuna worried about the consequences for his soul, but Krishna explained that if he always practiced devotion or yoga then his actions would not store up bad karma. So Krishna explains to Arjuna how to be still, how to meditate and be in harmony.

It is the habitual set of the mind towards God through spiritual practice, meditation, yoga, and prayer which ultimately counts and which can actually prevent bad karma from forming. This represents a spiritual breakthrough and is very similar to Christ's promise that whoever believes in him will have eternal life.

It really does not matter what form your devotion takes or in which tradition you choose to worship. There are different types of yoga so that even within the Hindu religion there are different paths, which you can take. The practice of trying to achieve enlightenment through worship is known as bhakti yoga. There is also jnana yoga that focuses on acquiring true knowledge of the self. Karma yoga is learning to detach yourself from habitual behaviour and to make decisions or actions based on non-selfish intentions. Other religions have their own "yogas" which are no less potent than those that Hinduism has developed.

The receiving of Holy Communion in Christianity is an extremely powerful force to combat the accumulation of bad karma. So too is the Muslim practice of prayer five times a day. Regular reading of scripture is central to most faiths as are hymns and chants. All of these religious practices have stood the test of time and have been developed for a reason. This is why the modern tendency to discard traditional religious practice is ultimately self-defeating. The New Age tendency to "get there in one" can produce a nihilistic frame of mind that leads nowhere. You can't take the religion out of Brahman – it is not given to man to realise it any other way.

ψ

Just as God does not belong to any one religion but to all, so does Brahman fit within the context of any belief system. You can follow all the tenets of Christianity and still accept that Brahman is the ultimate reality, the projection of God's consciousness that underlies everything. It is easy to see the moment when the Holy Spirit descended on Christ's apostles as a moment of Brahman realisation, when the veil was lifted for them and they saw every-thing as One. Ecstatic experiences in any religion can all be seen as instances when Brahman has been realised even if it is called by different names or interpreted through particular cultural filters. I would hazard that every single religious experience has at its core that particular feeling of wholeness, of everything being inter-connected and complete, and is accompanied by a feeling of deepest bliss and happiness. That is Brahman. It is a feeling of completely knowing your true self, of all fear falling away and deep intimacy with everything around you.

Sometimes Brahman can be sensed, but not deeply experienced, without any religious context. Artists through the generations will be the first to admit that something they could not quite identify was often inspiring them. When the poet William Wordsworth wrote that he sensed in nature "something more deeply interfused" that was his own Brahman moment, however fleeting. Wordsworth would not have called his insight "Brahman".

But then only the Indian mind has ever really articulated what these numinous, inspired moments have actually grasped. It is the Indian mind that has developed the metaphysics of these experiences and taught us how to go about calling up the sensing of Brahman and how to prolong its realisation.

These fleeting moments of Brahman realisation are important because they demand an explanation and are more common than reported. The uniting and causative factor in all these experiences is the sudden loss of the ego, the temporary loss of yourself like in a vacant daydream. With this loss of the ego comes the fading away of time-based consciousness and an indwelling of the atman (soul) in the present. This experience mimics the state achieved in meditation and is, if you like, a sampler of what can be experienced when the mind is fully at rest. So we all meditate at times even if it is very fleeting and inadvertent.

The question we should all be asking is that if all is Brahman then why don't we, as part of Brahman, constantly have awareness of this state? Why has God created a universe in which we should be blocked from seeing the truth?

The way to answer this question is actually to turn it around and ask why *should* we see the truth at all times? If we knew the totality of the truth at all times we would *be* God and nothing would exist except the personal God, the Isvara, at the centre of all. God has chosen to be aware of more than itself and to create a universe of many forms out of its universal awareness and evolutionary energy that we call Brahman. This Brahman is the extension of God's awareness into consciousness because to be conscious requires something to be conscious of. In other words, Brahman consciousness is a development of God's awareness of itself. The created order is like God's playground where it develops and learns through the hard knocks of living in a material world. We may feel that we are blocked from seeing the total truth but we are only agents of God's experience and it is not given to our individual atmans to see more than that given within our limiting sphere.

Another question we might ask then is that concerning spiritual insight. If God has cast our consciousness into its limiting sphere, why should we search for the truth at all and why should anyone be able to achieve deeper insight into the Brahman reality? You could almost imagine that the mystics and swamis, the saints and the avatars, have somehow cheated the system and seen into that which we are not really supposed to see! The first thing to realise, however, is that those who see Brahman do not see it in its totality. Only God can see that.

When in meditation we experience the *quality* of Brahman but not its wholeness. It is rather like knowing the sea by taking a cup of water of it and seeing what it tastes like.

Only God holds everything within total conscious embrace and we are always no more than fragments of God's experience. Even the ascended masters do not experience Brahman in its totality and it is clear that most seem to stay near our own mortal realm to help us make spiritual progress rather than further themselves.

A second point is to never lose sight of the fact that our own consciousness is Brahman awareness and cannot exist without it. Thus, if we are ultimately nothing but Brahman, how could we ever be concerned with anything less then taking our conscious witness to its full and being part of God's urge for the infinite expansion of its own awareness.

"Man cannot live by bread alone," said Christ, who knew that mankind would always feel the imperative to explore his environment including the dimension of meaning and spirit. It is not so much a case of *why* we seek spiritual insight, as we just can't help doing so. The only wonder is that some people try to deny their own curiosity and sense of search by saying they are "not religious". It is virtually impossible to be alive and not be religious. You are religious as soon as you ask the question "who am I and what is the purpose of life"? How you respond to that basic human question is up to you but just in asking it you are part of God's Brahman consciousness seeking to understand itself.

When you look up at the night sky and marvel at the stars you are the universe looking at itself. You are part of the universe knowing itself and it is at this point, where Brahman knows itself, where a special spot of creative energy is formed.

"Whatever is born, Arjuna, whether it moves or it moves not, know that it comes from a union of the field and the knower of the field."

Bhagavad Gita

When you know Brahman it is like a light being switched on in the darkness. It is a moment of pure bliss, an instant of illumination that is perfect love because the experience of Oneness is love. You are the knower of the field of Brahman so you are both Brahman and its self-reflection at the same time. By losing your illusory sense of self you see that what you really are is part of the extended super-consciousness of God and from it you can never be separated.

Bright but hidden, the Self dwells in the
heart.
Everything that moves, breathes, opens,
and closes
Lives in the Self. He is the source of love
And may be known through love but not
through thought.
He is the goal of life. Attain this goal!
Mundaka Upanishad

ψ

Karma, Atonement & Grace

The best way to get around sacred sites in India is to find a good taxi driver who will also act as a guide. In Goa I am very lucky and welcome the services of an elderly and knowledgeable driver who is also very religious. We visit a number of temples and at each one he shows me the process of worship that is more or less the same regardless of the god. It is humbling how the priests accept a Westerner's devotions without discrimination but such is the open-ended nature of Hinduism that it is a tradition without joining formalities or initiations. There is something very reassuring about a faith that is not puffed up, has no real priestly hierarchy (although it does have a priestly caste) and asks for no pledge towards a creed or a rigid statement of belief.

To the Hindus God is not in any way guarded or shielded behind dogma or interpreted by ecclesiastical niceties but is rather here and now for your experience by experiencing yourself.

Even the Brahmin caste, which was always supposed to be the guardian of the Hindu tradition, does not in any sense hold the key to valid religious experience. Nor do the Brahmin deter experimentation. Hinduism is, in a sense, anarchic and unpredictable and open to as many different interpretations as there are seekers after the truth. There is also in Hinduism, as I am about to discover, a capacity to shock. Don't go idly into a Hindu temple and make a prayer without expecting it to be answered. In India the veil is thin and raw Brahman hangs in the air with its power ready to break through.

My driver warns me that if you pray to Sai Baba in 80 per cent of cases you will experience a response of some kind. My driver is a particular devotee of the 19th century saint Sai Baba of Shirdi and he is most anxious that I visit a temple dedicated to him in

Panjim, the capital city of Goa. This is not the modern day Sai Baba who some claim to be the reincarnation of the Sai Baba of Shirdi, but an avatar whose life and miracles have had an enormous impact on the Hindu tradition and whose following is huge, not just in India. The Sai Baba temple in Panjim is tucked away and unpretentious. Inside the temple the image of Sai Baba is the familiar one known to all who have seen pictures of this saint where he sits with one leg over the other, a close fitting cap on his head and a thick lipped benign smile on his face. The statue of Sai Baba is peculiarly alive and somehow strangely luminescent.

Sitting cross-legged on the floor in front of the statue I asked Sai Baba to guide me towards Brahman realisation and to make my life take a new direction. I would be back here not once but twice before three months were out.

That night I was reflecting on my experiences around India and started to feel very down. I was disappointed with myself because I felt I had not done enough to make spiritual progress. I went to bed frankly quite fed up, but as I lay on my bed something started to come over me that completely changed the way I felt about myself. I felt a calming rush of reassurance, a sense of wholeness and purpose and complete oneness with the world. At the time I was not thinking in terms of a religious experience but went to sleep just warmed by how I felt. In the morning I awoke with this same intense feeling of everything being all right and it was only then that I thought about Sai Baba and wondered if there was a connection.

At this stage I gave it little more thought but Sai Baba had not finished with me yet.

ψ

Once we have realised Brahman and accepted fully that we are part of the ground consciousness of the universe, there comes a great "so what" moment? What do you do about it? This is the crisis point of the Advaitin and for a while the seeker might feel alone with an almost nihilistic approach to mortal life. If we are all part of the One and there is no such thing as the death of our consciousness then what actually is the point of life on earth? Why, even, would we need to feel responsible for our actions if the physical domain is no more than Maya, an impermanent reality that is a projection of Brahman? You will hear some neo-Advaitins say that the answer to realising that all is Brahman, is to do nothing. There is nothing to do; all is perfect and present in the now. This response to Brahman is a result of getting there too quickly, of choosing a direct path to Advaita rather than undergoing a long period of disciplined study, instruction, meditation and mind training. There is a crisis in neo-Advaitism that has come about by a lazy approach to religion in the West that wants enlightenment without spirituality and discipline.

Realising Brahman can indeed seem a very abstract satisfaction. The problem in the West, is that seekers have taken the religion out of Advaita and been left with a cold metaphysical theory. You cannot get to Brahman realisation without the tried and trusted pathways of religious study and practice. This does not mean you have to become a Hindu but you will only see into Brahman through spiritual practice. This is why the Hindu faith has developed its vast panoply of gods with all their colour, humanity and ability to inspire distinct spiritualities. For most Hindus, Brahman realisation lies at the back of their religious feelings but they want something more personal, more tangible and more human related to inspire their spiritual lives.

There is nothing wrong with this. You will never hear a fully realised soul like Sai Baba or Ramakrishnan decry forms of Hindu worship. This is because they understand that you have to start somewhere and that for all the wonderful variety and drama in the Hindu pantheon, every god relates back to the One. Hindu gods are a product of the religious imagination, a set of human representations of how the One becomes the many.

But if Brahman realisation seems such abstract and high philosophy how can it be lived and how does it inform us to act? A priest I met painting icons at Glastonbury Abbey who was a convert to the orthodox Christian church, gave the answer to me. He told me that it could all be summed up in one word – atonement. He explained that the whole motivation for what we do should, at all times, be to correct or atone for the negative actions ("sins") which we are responsible for in this life and in previous lives.

Life is not about being a "success", achieving happiness or amassing lots of money. It is not about glory, power or fame. Your meaning is never less than being a fragment of God's consciousness, part of the ultimate experiencing itself. All is Brahman and our mortal existence is so that we experience things and take actions. It is only the totality of our karmic record which counts and the figuring out of what is pure, positive (good) or pertaining to the divine, as opposed to that which is bad, negative (evil) and which is not the nature of the divine.

As we work through our karmic reality we are in essence God experiencing and testing its own nature to the extreme. The conscious act of addressing negative experiences or actions by replacing it with a positive experience or action is called atonement and it is this dynamic alone which should power and direct all our mortal life. In Eastern religion this principle of atonement is well understood but it is driven by a deep-seated belief in the existence of karma without an understanding of which it is impossible ever to understand yourself let alone experience Brahman.

What is this terrible thing called "karma"? Both Hindu and Buddhist tradition tells us in no uncertain terms that karma is our life actions carried over into our next reincarnation. Our next reincarnation is determined because we carry karma that has not been "worked out" and the object is to address this bad karma in a new life. It is a daunting prospect because it is telling us that our past is forever with us, not just the past of our present life but also the past of all our previous lives put together.

Why should that be? And what is bad karma? We talk about "sins" but where is the ultimate moral reference that determines what is a sin and what is just a consequence of being human?

Take a step back and think again about karma and perhaps it is not such an awful condition. If God is experiencing itself through us then it is feeling itself through our lives and determining what is "good" (perfect and complete) against what is "bad" (negative and imperfect) over the course of the unfolding of the universe. There is no ultimate "good" and "bad" until God has identified its true nature through experience. So what we mean by "good" is God's total realisation of itself, as opposed to "bad" which means those actions or thoughts that do not pertain to the nature of God.

You are part of God working this out and it is a dynamic process of infinite self-realisation that is the very nature of the Godhead and which is still taking place. So is karma so difficult to understand after all? What you have done and what you are doing in this life is part of God's Brahman consciousness and it is all remembered in God's timeless memory of experience.

For God to understand and complete its experiential reality it has to evolve and carry forward all consciousness until it is fully worked out and all experience made perfect through a process of awareness and correction. It is not that you are so bad you have to be reborn again to learn a lesson. It is that God is trying to experience itself in its totality through material existence and that your life is part of this long, agonising dynamic towards perfection.

Experience your karma. I believe most people know their own karma without ever really thinking about it. We have inner feelings, hints, almost memories that pertain to a previous existence. It is what gives us our "flavour", that ultimate individuality that is something far and above our genetic inheritance that, of course, helps determine our full human nature.

Our karma is carried by our soul, our "atman", that splinter of Brahman that is our unitary inheritance with God. Our karma is carried forward because it is God carrying it forward within itself to live out the experience to its full and perfect conclusion. The universe is God's experience of itself in material form and you are part of that experience. If God simply absorbed each mortal existence into itself it would be imperfect (indigestible) and without the ultimate resolution of experience which God seeks. So our individual identities come back to confront themselves again and, over and over, experience existence until they become perfect with the God nature. It is God discovering God in its fullness and karma in its entirety is the process working itself out until all is complete.

It is very important, liberating in a sense, to embrace your karma and be in love with it. Do not be downtrodden by the "sin" you carry with you but look upon it as part of God's experience of itself and see your life as a work in progress. You are part of God looking at itself and trying to become the perfect mirror in which God sees itself in its fullest expression. Take your karma and wrestle with it, witness it and try to find a way to redeem that which you sense is negative or "bad". Work on it all the time. Atonement is at the centre of all religions because they all, in their different ways, recognise that it is how you have dealt with your karma (or "sin" if you prefer) which will determine your soul path upon death.

In the Tibetan Book of the Dead the whole teaching is aimed at instruction about how to prepare for death because the Buddhists know that it is what constitutes your total karma and your acknowledgment and atonement of which that will shape your journey once you die. In Christianity the whole purpose of Christ's sacrifice on the cross is to provide a way of atonement for our bad karma (sins) so that we may be assisted on our path towards perfection. The Hindus immerse themselves in the Ganges with the same inner determination to wash away their limitations so that they may achieve moksha and liberation from the cycle of re-birth.

To know your karma is to really know your individual atman or soul self. At all times, the atman is part of Brahman but in its separate distinctiveness it is coloured, or should we say flavoured, by its total conscious experience. Thus, Brahman is individuated by our separate karmas all working themselves out until the conclusion of God's experiment with itself as universe. We see karma all around us but we do not really acknowledge it for what it is.

Is it not strange how different siblings can be even though they share mostly common genes? The reason is because we all carry a unique imprint of different lives and are in the fullest sense very special, separate cargoes of conscious experiences. Some people today seek to know their karma through the process known as "soul regression" where a therapist is able to trigger your memory of a previous life or lives. There are those, we hear, who have such memory of previous lives they are able to recount in detail previous life experiences or even born able to speak in different languages. But I believe that we have an innate sense of our own past lives which expresses itself at odd moments and which can surface in dreams.

In meditation, or even just a quiet reflective moment, we can sometimes obtain a very clear idea of ourselves as a kind of karmic filter through which we are experiencing Brahman. This "through a glass darkly" sense of experiencing the truth is the very nature of karma – it is the accumulated material entrapment through which consciousness is being made to travel before the fog clears and it realises itself.

Let us take a step back. Could it be that what we call karma is just conscience by another name? Do we humans have some massive hang-up on guilt that is just a result of social conditioning and that we have invented elaborate means of dealing with it from concepts of heaven and hell, original sin, redemption, atonement and carried forward karma? We have to cross this bridge of sin/karma before we can move forward and be quite plain of what we are talking about.

We all know that what we categorise as sins or "negative behaviour" often have their origins in circumstance rather than any path or course of action which we actually prefer to make. The soldier who kills a man in battle has been ordered to do so and it seems unfair to some people that he should carry forward bad karma as someone who has committed a sin. We may all falter in one way or another but what decides what is bad or good karma? To take the doctrine of karma to its literal limit means that we can make one slip and are reincarnated next time as a pig or whatever to teach us a lesson. Really? This is the point at which we have to realise that all religions have their tub thumping moralisers and pulpit bashing extremists and that it is a side-effect of faith that some will hijack the spiritual search in the name of morality as they decree it. Even in the gentle religions of the East this high moral tone can be heard and there is something about it that grates and which doesn't quite add up.

A God which incarnates itself and thus limits itself into material universe does not then go about punishing its splinters who don't conform to a perfection that has been defined by priests who themselves are capable of weakness. I don't go quite as far as the philosopher who called morality "the private joke of mankind" but neither can Jesus' Ten Commandments or the Buddha's Eightfold Path be the whole story. We need a much bigger picture than that and preferably one that reconciles moral absolutes with circumstantial relatives. When reactionaries condemn our age for its "moral relativeness" they are simply choosing to ignore the realities and details of life. When the existentialists proclaim that there is no absolute good or sin, they were right. After all, Jesus said, "let him who is without sin cast the first stone."

But what the existentialists did not pause to consider is that the good and bad of things is in the process of being worked out. Just as galaxies form, planetary systems evolve and life emerges so too is the moral universe in the process of figuring itself out. The universe is not in some static state with moral absolutes already determined.

God, through its projected Brahman consciousness is experiencing itself through the multiplicity of life forms locked in all the chance and circumstance of material existence. There is a theory, expounded in the book by Jack Miles, "Christ, A Crisis In The Life of God", that God fully manifested itself on earth through the incarnate Christ as a kind of apology to man that we are bound by our material fate never to be fully capable of perfect virtue and that we need an advocate or ameliorator who acts as a "propitiation for our sins". Put another way, the intervention of a Christ is God revising the order of things as a result of its experience so far.

This idea of God not as a static being but as an evolving force is increasingly accepted amongst philosophers. Even if God and Brahman exist outside of time we must conclude that God does live in time as much as it is living its consciousness through its incarnation in a material world. God is evolving, learning and even reacting just as we do ourselves for our own lives are its lives.

To return to the question of karma we can see that our individual souls' karmas are just part of God's memory because our souls are inseparable from Brahman consciousness. All experience is carried forward because Brahman is timeless and nothing is ever forgotten or left undone. We have to accept the idea that our reincarnations of our karmic selves must number in their thousands, as the sages of the East have always informed us. Given the enormous spans of time over which the universe is evolving we should perhaps not be surprised by this karmic longevity. It is clear upon the most basic reading of religious history that very few humans have ever achieved moksha or nirvana and that our souls are at the very earliest stages of karmic development. Those who have achieved both the knowledge of Brahman and the total renunciation of self (freedom from sin) are those who are now empowered within Brahman and can act as guides (some call them angels) to us as we try to reach higher. But the overwhelming majority of us will be reincarnated again after the death of this lifetime to once again try and work through the karmic load we carry with us.

Why is it so difficult to break out of our karmic shackles and achieve moksha or nirvana?

One of the terrible realities of karma is that our karmic selves are self-re-enforcing and lead us not only to repeatedly confront past karma but also actually to live it over and over again. Aldous Huxley once said, "the things that happen to people are like the people they happen to." This was another way of saying our karma tends us towards repeating karma of the same type. Thus, if you were a thief in a previous life you are quite likely to feel some degree of urge to pilfer in your present world.

This is hard graft but it reflects the deeply felt notion that the universe is just one vast karmic storyline of actions and reactions, and that all events are linked in a great consequential chain. It is not until you can overcome negative, or "immoral" or "selfish non Brahman-conscious acts or thoughts" that you can resolve your entire karmic burden and ascend towards the centre of the Godhead.

It is only when the individual soul, or "atman", fully realises that it is Brahman and does something about it by renouncing material self (and thus "sin") that the process of you as part of God's self-realisation is complete and the bliss of perfection is obtained.

Karma is a "momentum towards" certain actions or behaviour. It is more than the sum of our past actions, it is also a determinant of likely future actions. To arrest this karmic momentum and stop it is immensely difficult and is why very few people have achieved release from the cycle of death and rebirth. If one had to make a guess at how many individual human souls have achieved moksha or nirvana it would be difficult to imagine the figure at more than a few thousand. That is how far away mankind is from realising its true nature and using that knowledge to liberate its great charge of souls into a higher level of Brahman consciousness. Mankind is a work in progress and its path towards self-discovery is a long one. Perhaps it will not be until the global population has stabilised or even falls before any real progress is made towards working out the total human karma.

Remember that we are all one in Brahman consciousness and our individual atman souls are, from God's point of view, seen as one with itself. To get too hung up on your own karma is to allow the ego back into the picture. True Brahman awareness comes through losing the sense of identity with the ego or "mind" and realising that you are the consciousness of Brahman and nothing else. So, although we are truly individuated in Brahman and distinct souls carrying karma of past lives we are ultimately all one with a God who sees the big picture.

Unless God had this sense of the whole rather than the individual then life on this Earth would make little sense. How can you make sense of an earthquake that suddenly kills 10,000 people indiscriminately and cuts off their possibility of any karmic advancement unless God sees things in the round? God carries the whole karmic load with itself – the karma of all human experience belongs to it and not to us. Thus to get obsessed with your own karma is misjudged because it is a tiny part of a universal karma which belongs to God.

We also have no real idea of how individual karmas are reincarnated. Personally I believe the process is complex and highly subtle and completely beyond our ability to understand. I don't think the same experience happens to every soul, and I believe there are different levels or degrees to which the soul is re-absorbed into Brahman upon mortal death.

Realisation of Brahman during earthly life is, as the Upanishads frequently tell us, the key to escaping the cycle of rebirth and Brahman-realised souls will be better informed as they pass through the portal of death. But you can realise Brahman and still carry bad karma, so exactly what happens to us then is a mystery. I would guess that just to realise Brahman intellectually is not enough. What would ultimately be decisive is if the soul had realised Brahman at the deepest spiritual level of discovery and that in finding perfect union with the ground of Being all ego, and thus all karma, had been worked out or released. This is the heart of Brahman realisation and its relationship to karma. By fully realising Brahman there can only be one result, which is the end of identification with the ego, or mind, and thereby releasing the mortal sense sheath which was the very cause of any karma in the first place.

ψ

The Vedantic system is not a creed and never tends towards dogma of any kind. In fact, there is no one Vedanta but a generally shared philosophy that has developed its many branches over time. Perhaps the most fundamental disagreement amongst Vedantists is the non-dual monist theology of Shankara's Advaita and the theist teachings of Ramajuna. This is really the age-old argument of whether there is a personal or impersonal God. The classic advaitin stance is that there is no separation between spirit and matter, that all is one with God. On the face of it that looks like saying there is no personal god. Ramajuna disagreed with Shankara and allowed for the worship of a personal god that was not distinct from Brahman but, perhaps, its highest manifestation. These distinctions, which you will read in theology books about personal and impersonal gods, are now looking very limited in their understanding.

Many interpreters of sages like Shankara and Ramajuna have over-simplified what was being said by both and in doing so fallen from that knife edge of understanding which is required to see beyond the limitations of mere words.

God is personal and impersonal at the same time depending on the depth that you have attained in seeking the divine. At what we may call the general, everyday level, God is impersonal, allowing the forces of the creation to carry the universe along its evolutionary path.

What happens in the world will often seem no more than chance and God seems nowhere to be seen. But those cognizant of Brahman appreciate that God is everywhere at all times and that there is no other reality that the eternal consciousness of God.

To know (better still, to feel) that you are part of this God consciousness we call Brahman is to render the question of a personal god meaningless. God is as personal as you are as long as you find it. To truly know yourself is to know God because you are inseparable from God. Thus when you seek a personal relationship with God through prayer or actions you are essentially addressing yourself and what answers your prayers is the God within you. Christians have insisted that the answering of prayers is an act of grace on God's behalf. But what is grace? The grace has been "discovered" rather than "given" because the person praying has touched God through his or her spiritual outreach. It is like the closing of a circle.

Discover that you are part of God through realisation of Brahman consciousness and God's powers of creation, of altering reality, become yours. This is how the religious greats through the centuries have been able to perform miracles. Not because they have been *handed* some special power but because they have reached there themselves and seen that the ability to take actions and create and change things comes from understanding that consciousness is the source of all power.

Prayer is one form of reaching out to God and prayer when answered is another way of closing the circle and discovering that God is within you. Prayer is answered not because there is a dualist response between prayer and God but because you have discovered God within and you are answering the prayer yourself.

This may sound shocking to the conventionally religious standpoint which sees God as wholly separate from self but the non-dualist who realises that there is only the one Brahman reality, only sees the unitive state and looks inward rather than outward to find God. Jesus said: "The Kingdom of Heaven is within you." "Look inward, find Brahman, know that you are part of Brahman, and the power of Brahman is with you," Jesus may equally have said.

Prayer can be intermediated, however, and if it wasn't the case, most of us would never have our prayers answered. Within Brahman higher, fully realised souls continue their existence as helpers of mankind as we struggle to make spiritual progress. Higher spirits can be angels, ascended masters and saints like a Sai Baba or Ramakrishnan. In the Christian tradition it is often the Virgin Mary who is called upon as an intermediary and Jesus himself, of course, is another agency through which we try to reach God. The level at which we achieve this intermediation depends upon our own spiritual status, on our karma and depth of understanding of Brahman. The need for most of us to have this personalised form of spirituality is strong and is very evident in Hinduism, with its enormous range of god images which help the seeker see into Brahman and create the feedback loop which answers prayers through self realisation. It really does not matter which form your God worship takes. Jesus called God the "Father", Ramakrishna worshipped through the Hindu mother goddess Kali and similarly, many Christians find the potency of

Marian worship irresistible. The Buddhists, too, are familiar with the importance of having your own God image through which you seek the Eternal. The Tibetan Book of the Dead is quite explicit in emphasising the importance of focusing on your particular God image at the time of your passing so that you make the most opportune progress in the afterlife.

The importance of having your own god image cannot be over-stated. I would really challenge the idea that you can realise Brahman in some kind of secular, non-religious way. Your god image acts to focus your spirituality and give it a cutting edge. It is what changes your sight, colours your mind and induces a change in your feelings. Your god image is also how you are drawn out of yourself so that you leave behind the ego and bear witness to a wider reality. It matters little what god image you choose but what is important is that it is personal and highly evocative to you. Most of us choose god images at the centre of world religions like a Jesus or Krishna but others attach themselves to various saints, holy men and women, angels or avatars.

Your god image must never be seen in isolation but as part of the wider Brahman reality. The god image is a way of being guided into this reality and making you realise that you are part of it. Some people believe we all have our own guardian angel but even if you chose this as your god image you must picture the angel as existing within Brahman, like a bright spot within the Brahman field.

Experience seems to show that all fully realised souls like to help us and love to be asked to assist us in various ways. The act of prayer is hugely powerful and you should choose your thoughts and wishes carefully before addressing your personal god image. Prayer is often answered in strange ways and if you ask for one thing you are quite likely to receive something completely different. The reason is that God knows what you really need, not simply what you think you need, at the time of your prayer.

Once I was visiting the Marian shrine at Walsingham in England and before a blessing from the waters of the holy well the priest warned the worshippers that prayers were frequently answered here but often not in the way people expected. Later that same day I was alone in the shrine when a shield bearing the sign of the Cross Keys fell off the wall at my feet. The Cross Keys are the symbol of St Peter to whom Jesus gave the keys to the kingdom of heaven. But I have never fully understood the meaning of that event to me.

I don't think we fully understand the mechanism by which prayers are answered or are even able to pray properly most of the time. I suspect that we are made to answer the prayer ourselves in some way by being shown who we really are.

Prayer illuminates us because it draws us out of ourselves and heightens our consciousness. Prayer should really be the same as meditation accept that we ask for help through intermediation. It is perfectly valid to ask for help but never forget that you are one with Brahman and therefore one with the spirit to whom you are praying. Do not see a difference between you and your god image but, instead, imagine you are one with that spirit and then its benign powers will flow into you.

The idea of any kind of spiritual discipline is increasingly alien in the modern world. People in the West seem to want to achieve insight without any effort and do not regard regular attendance at a place of worship or any devotional practice as necessary or relevant. This is a great mistake.

If there were short cuts to God, life would indeed be easy but that is not how Brahman has laid out its great matrix of creation. The universe is process and God's unfolding consciousness can only progress because it realises itself through resistance with the material world. We are that consciousness pushing to witness itself, yearning to transcend limitation and gain higher reali-sation. God is great but gets greater all the time as its experiential dimension is pushed ever further through us and all conscious creation.

So whoever said life was supposed to be easy? It is all effort and struggle and there is certainly no self-realisation without purpose and the willingness to work at it. You would struggle to find an example of a saint or other fully realised spirit who had not achieved any degree of enlightenment without years of rigorous spiritual practice. This is because to rid yourself of ego and develop Brahman awareness is difficult and requires a single-mindedness and self-discipline which most of us struggle to achieve.

The modern world with its torrents of distractions, tasks and duties is not conducive to spiritual disciplines and we really have to envy those holy men in India who spend their days behind the walls of their ashrams isolated from the 21st century with nothing else to do but make spiritual advancement. But try we must and it doesn't really matter which path you choose so long as it is a well-trodden one and preferably prescribed for you by a guru or teacher.

There are those who will read religious texts each day and intersperse this with prayer or meditation. There are ascetic exercises like fasting or enduring other physical discomforts. There is public or collective worship and prayer that is perhaps highly underestimated these days. What matters is the regularity of the practice and the intention of the seeker. You cannot go through the motions with religion. There has to be real intent and purpose. You have to know what you are trying to do and have the intellectual framework to interpret what you experience. Talking with a minister of the Church once he was most interested in what I was reading, for this, he thought, was most important with reference to the spiritual search.

It is certainly possible to experience Brahman intuitively but you will never know what you are experiencing until you have read about it. Reading the Upanishads is essential, for nowhere else is Brahman described so perfectly. The many texts and commentaries on Vedanta and Advaita can be read over and over again. Many Hindus repeatedly read the Bhagavad Gita whose story setting of the Vedantic teachings is very compelling. I once read the entire Bible over a year by reading a set portion every day. I wish I could remember all that I had read but I realise that equally important as content was the daily discipline of reading a certain amount.

It is the changing of your daily habits and routine that counts – that prescribing of a certain time for the loss of ego, for contemplation of meaning and the striving for God. In time you will find that you have changed and new experiences come to you. Ramakrishna prayed to Kali for enlightenment over many years before he thought he made a breakthrough. But ultimately your conscious discipline and search has pre-disposed yourself to *see* and Brahman will eventually begin to open up before you.

The greatest spiritual tool is meditation and all pundits in both Buddhism and Hinduism advocate its practice. Meditation can lead to the highest state of consciousness we can achieve in our mortal form apart from those extreme states of bliss experienced in the trance-like state known in Hinduism as samadhi. Meditation, practiced properly, is a state of extreme conscious awareness in a split second of time. It is the very now-ness that we try to achieve in meditation that is key. To experience the Brahman reality we need to be super-conscious of the very moment before us and to eliminate all awareness of anything beyond this moment.

This is not the place to describe how to meditate because there have been enough books on that. I would, however, argue that once you have experienced these super-now moments in meditation there is no reason why you cannot use them to focus your non-meditational mind in the same way. Living in the present is a mind-practice which can be learned and one which will help you be aware of Brahman at all times and not just when the ego is switched off. Meditation is a means to an end and not an end in itself. After we have been meditating we still have to live in the "real world" and we should ask ourselves what good has our meditation done and how will it help us in our mortal form? The answer is that you carry the awareness gained in meditation into your everyday life and stay sharpened to the moment at all times. Worrying about the past or the future is your greatest waste of time. Living in the moment makes the world glow with purpose and "rightness" because you are living the timeless quality of Brahman, the true reality that is bliss.

ψ

It was a long journey by road to reach Sai Baba's hometown of Shirdi. Overnight I travel by sleeper-coach across the Western Ghats from Goa to Pune and the next day I take a three-hour bus journey deep into Maharastra to arrive in Shirdi in the baking heat of midday. The pilgrimage to do dharsan at Sai Baba's shrine in Shirdi is big business in this part of India. Followers of Sai Baba pack my bus and seem completely non-plussed that a foreigner is amongst them. In Shirdi the size of the crowds comes as a surprise and I realise that this is not going to be one of those quiet, contemplative pilgrimages but more of a mad scrummage and something just to get through. Inside Sai Baba's shrine the faithful are ushered like cattle along gangways, but the order breaks down when you finally reach the inner sanctum there to look upon that distinctive face, garlanded with flowers and smiling on the mad scrabble beneath his image.

Is Sai Baba really here with us? There is certainly a very strong sense of presence but this whole experience is not one of receiving something but rather of asking to be guided and giving thanks. Hindus are not afraid of asking for favours in their prayers but a more potent offering perhaps is to say thank you for what you have and simply to make an acknowledgement of your search. Sai Baba once expressed surprise and gratitude when one of his many visitors asked help to see Brahman rather than a request for personal favours that was the norm. I am wary and, to be honest, slightly afraid, of Sai Baba so I don't ask for anything so much as to be guided as he sees best.

These were dark days for me in Shirdi and Pune and I felt oppressed as though Sai Baba was leading me towards some kind of karmic crisis or confrontation.

A spiritual friend back in England had warned me that I would soon face some moment of inner disturbance. I can't help feeling that Sai Baba reads you like a book and when you appeal to him he sees you like a vast karmic map and understands where the contours are pointing. It is a bit like being in church and looking at the rest of the congregation and feeling that they are all better people than you are and that you don't deserve to be there! I was glad to get out of Shirdi because the experience had not been what I wanted but I knew deep down that my shadow had for a moment passed over a very keen spiritual eye.

Once you have acknowledged Brahman there is nothing that seems impossible any more. Brahman is latent power there to be directed by God or those fully realised souls whose intimacy with this great force enables them to use it. Sai Baba's miracles were many and they are well attested to by so many different people during his lifetime that it strains credulity to believe they were all made up mumbo jumbo.

So I was not exactly surprised when I saw the eyes of his image move when I was back at his temple in Panjim. My partner and I are standing alone in front of the statue and his eyes are clearly glancing from side to side scrutinising us. We both see it together. We stand in awe and my partner is shaking and in tears. This solid stone statue is alive with the power of Brahman and Sai Baba's soul is still at work here on Earth.

We don't tell anyone what we saw but I get the impression

that if you were to tell any of the other Sai Baba faithful that they would hardly be surprised. In India miracles are not so much exceptional as expected. If you are an enlightened soul then to religious Indians it would be a matter of course that you have supernatural powers to some degree.

For me Sai Baba's acknowledgement was more of a puzzle than an inspiration. Perhaps he was saying that I don't need him and just to journey forth the way you are doing? Having brought my karma into focus it was up to me to do something about it.

All religious experience is always about moments of self-realisation. You see into infinity be seeing deeper into yourself.

"Know Yourself" it said at the entrance to the Delphic Oracle in Greece.

Pilgrimage, like the trip I made to Shirdi, does not necessarily lead to joy but sometimes through pain and anguish to truth. By making the outward journey you complete an inward journey and the physical discomfort of travelling is matched by an interior discomfort of changed priorities, karmic angst and truths hard learned.

ψ

What Sees That?
The Science Of Brahman

There is no point trying to limit yourself in the search for truth. It will not do to say "science is the only way" or that some fundamentalist religious path has all the answers. You have to be an everyman, a polymath, someone brave enough to open themselves to the whole welter of human experience and try to take of much as it in as possible.

Truth is a tantalising mist that lies somewhere between the lands of science, religious experience and artistic insight. Most people are too happy to live on their little ego island with a cosy self-image as a science type, a follower of whatever identity-reinforcing tribal belief system, an arty type or perhaps someone who just likes jazz!

In the Indian tradition you won't find so much of this human narrowness but instead, a more curious and inclusive way of looking at the world.

The Vedas actually encouraged a scientific approach to the world while being no less spiritually inspiring. The Buddha made no claims and instead just invited people to follow a path of enquiry. Modern Indians include some of the best software scientists in the world but are equally adept at taking advice from holy men and astrologers. Where is the problem? All we need to do is drop the ego and be still. Take everything in and remain curious for life.

It was not any religion which brought me to believe in God but, in fact, a small book on science. I had just finished my degree studies in human evolution and prehistory when I read Isaac Asimov's "The Wellsprings of Life" and was so awed at the fantastic complexity of the biochemistry here on Earth that it defied credulity to think that there was not design inherent in it all.

It is our lost sense of wonder that bedevils us all. The very existence of consciousness is the greatest and most wonderful thing of all. Even before my encounter with Asimov it was science rather than faith that inspired my philosophical musings about reality.

As a sixteen year old I was dwelling upon the nature of awareness or consciousness and suddenly fell into one of those sweet states that always seem to accompany a momentary glimpse of something beyond. I saw two particles colliding together and realised that each were "conscious" of the impact. It seemed to me that consciousness was just a matter of degree and that even at the sub-atomic level all is awareness. Two particles bumping together is just the first stage of an ordering process in the universe, of the process towards greater complexity that eventually results in life forms and higher states of consciousness.

Of course, with Brahman awareness the conviction that particles are "aware" is reinforced because this conscious substrate is conscious of everything at all times. Everything that happens, right down to the impact of two elementary particles, is witnessed by the conscious mirror of Brahman. Another way of saying this is that everything is experienced in the mind of God and so everything is the subject of conscious witness. But we have to go even further than this.

In Advaitin philosophy the physical world is created by Brahman through Maya and is thus a projection of Brahman itself. There is no duality between pure consciousness (call it "spirit" if you like) and conscious forms, whether microscopic or mammal-sized, in the material world. The question thus arises of whether we can find an echo of this Universal Oneness glimpsed in Eastern philosophy with the contemporary theories of modern science.

ψ

The subatomic or quantum world is probably the best place to look for evidence of the conscious substrate to the universe that we call Brahman. Quantum physics is the leading edge of scientific enquiry and today we see this area of research is where the boundaries of physics and philosophy seem very indistinct.

Scientists don't usually like to be associated with religious ideas but it is striking how many physicists seeking clues to the ultimate nature of matter have recently been responsive to the wisdom teachings of India. Scientific enquiry is showing signs of achieving some kind of accommodation with spiritual insight.

The divide that opened up between scientific rationalism and religious experience has been the enemy of all seekers after the truth. This was not always the case. In the ancient world there was no conflict between scientific investigation and religious exploration. Philosophers from Plato to Wittengenstein saw science and religion as two sides of the same coin. The natural science philosophers like Isaac Newton pursued both scientific and mystical lines of examining reality. The divide between science and religion only really opened up after the so-called Age of Reason in the 18th century and was at its most extreme in the rampant materialism of the following two centuries. Today, however, the good news is that we may be coming full circle with the search for the ultimate theory of matter leading some scientists back to an appreciation of religious philosophy, metaphysics and wisdom teachings.

The beginnings of scientists' new curiosity in religious teachings have their origin in 20th century advances in particle physics and the gaining of a deeper understanding of how the world works at the quantum level. Einstein's breakthroughs in quantum theory and relativity made the world seem a very weird place. Suddenly, old certainties were gone and the world had to come to terms with a reality that seemed uncertain, contingent on how it was being observed, neither wave nor particle and wrapped up in extra dimensions of space-time that we could not experience ourselves. Time itself was no longer a fixed quantity but varied according to speed and standpoint.

More disturbing still was the problem that still exists today that the rules of the quantum world are at variance with those that describe the larger macro world of which we are aware. Things just don't add up.

Ever since Einstein, the physicists have struggled to find a way to reconcile the reality they could demonstrate at the quantum level and the bigger picture world that was effectively described by Newton. The problem is that very strange things are happening at the quantum level that seem to merit a new understanding of how the universe fits together.

At the subatomic level, matter, we learn, has no permanent reality but is best seen as bundles of energy with no more than a statistical probability of being in one state or another. Only the act of observing a particle "fixes" it as a measurable unit. Observing means placing one's consciousness on something. The interrelationship between consciousness and creation is thereby laid bare. Moreover, the state of each particle seems to be determined not by local cause-and-effect but by non-local factors throughout the universe.

Each particle is not understandable without knowledge of the whole. In the theories put forward by the physicist David Bohm there may even be an "implicate order" in which each part of the material world contains the whole and that matter and consciousness are in some way "enfolded" together. In other words, everything is interconnected as One – just as the Eastern mystics have always been telling us.

"..... both in relativity theory and quantum theory, notions implying the undivided wholeness of the universe would provide a more orderly way of considering the general nature of reality."

David Bohm "Wholeness and the Implicate Order"

The best illustration of the strange enfolded world which exists at the quantum level is the phenomenon of "remote attraction" or, as it is sometimes called, "non-locality", "entanglement" or "attraction at a distance".

Einstein said that if two quantum particles become entangled they would continue to correspond to each other even if they have been split apart by vast distances. Subsequent experiments have shown that this is true. Classically, two particles bonded in a symmetrical spin state will reflect each other's state even if they are split apart. Reverse the state of spin of the one particle and the other will instantly (faster than the speed of light) also reverse its spin. The experiment has been performed many times and the results are the same.

What is the connection between the two particles that enables them to "stay in touch" even when separated? The implications of remote attraction are profound. If there is interconnectedness at the quantum level could it also exist at the macro level of living systems, solar systems and galaxies? It is as though the universe is one gigantic hologram, a projection of consciousness and matter that retains its wholeness from any perspective.

Science has no answer to the mystery of entanglement and has sometimes given the impression of being embarrassed by the phenomenon, preferring it to go away. By the beginning of the 21st century, however, there was a noticeable and welcome shift in the way physicists were approaching the problem.

Any academic discipline is by nature cautious, moves forward gradually through the publication of demonstrable truths reviewed critically within its peer group. To step outside this self-examining process is not only to threaten the status quo but it can also threaten the careers of individuals who threaten to rock the boat. But physicists are getting braver. There is a growing feeling amongst physicists that something is clearly missing and that the only way to find the answer is to throw their old approaches up in the air and dare to think the unthinkable.

Physicists now talk in terms of reality as being something highly subtle, consisting of wave fronts in high dimensional space. The three dimensional space we think we see is an illusion. Matter is best seen as a very high-energy form brought about by the collapse of the wave. This new thinking has been brought about by the crying need to explain nonlocality.

"The nonlocality of quantum physics might be our window into this deeper level of reality."

David Z Albert and Riva Galchen

in Scientific American, March 2009

This willingness to seek new ways of looking at physical reality has been a long time coming. There were any number of hints during the last 150 years or so that our scientific understanding of the universe was incomplete unless it took account of deeper philosophical insights.

Einstein himself believed that scientific progress came first through insight and only secondly through experimental and mathematical proof. Countless writers and thinkers from H.P. Blavatsky to Teilhard de Chardin and Rene Guenon have been pointing the way to a deeper, more holistic view of the universe as an inter-connected whole which cannot be understood without grasping the big picture.

A breakthrough was Fritjof Capra's book "The Tao of Physics" first published in 1975, which started the paradigm shift towards an outlook of enquiry embracing both quantum reality and the spiritual.

Serious scientists like Roger Penrose and Brian Greene then opened up the strangeness of quantum physics to a wider audience and seemed to leave the door open to philosophical enquiry.

Roger Penrose is interested in the relationship between quantum reality and consciousness and in "The Emperor's New

Mind" he speculated:

"Might a quantum world be *required* (his italics) so that thinking, perceiving creatures, such as ourselves, can be constructed from its substance?"

Greene wrote about string theory in his book called "The Elegant Universe" that what we know as space, time and dimension may not be the way we should define the universe. "Rather, they are convenient notions that emerge from a more basic, atavistic, and primary state."

It is very noticeable how the serious scientists in their speculations about quantum reality never quite go so far as to talk about the possibility of a background field of consciousness which acts as the common substrate against which all phenomenon occur. But one cannot help but think that they are privately toying with the idea.

Many of these scientists are now versed in the ideas of Eastern philosophy and there is little doubt that their enquiries are being informed by what they have gleaned from the Hindu and Buddhist teachings.

Even so, scientists are very reluctant to embrace the full implications of what they have discovered at the quantum level. The evidence for remote attraction has truly enormous philosophic implications but the scientists seem happy to play it down.

This also irked Fritjof Capra when he wrote in The Tao of Physics:

"Although their [scientists] theories are leading to a world view which is similar to that of the mystics, it is striking how little this has affected the attitudes of most scientists. ... most of today's physicists do not seem to realise the philosophical, cultural and spiritual implications of their theories."

ψ

Those with Brahman awareness will not be surprised by what the physicists have discovered about remote attraction. Particles can influence each other over a distance because they exist within the Oneness of Brahman consciousness and everything is interlinked because all is One.

It may be that it is only at the quantum level that Brahman can be demonstrated scientifically. How strange that what physicists are trying to discover in their huge particle accelerators is the same that Eastern mystics have been talking about for generations! The scientific process, of course, cannot rely upon spiritual insight to base its conclusions but it could borrow from those insights to construct a working hypothesis. Is it possible that all material phenomenon take place against a universal substrate of pure consciousness? The scientists could go even further and hypothesise that all material phenomenon are the *product* of a universal consciousness. Occam's Razor will always be invoked to prevent too much speculation in science but at present a unified theory of how consciousness and the phenomenal world interact requires some imagination.

Physicists already accept that the act of observation alters reality in some strange way or perhaps, "fixes" reality. Without observation the world at the quantum level is in an interminable flux-like state where quantum particles merely possess a possibility or probability of being in one position or another. This fact could be a clue as to how consciousness is the determinant in what we see as reality. It is important to try and describe exactly what we mean here.

There is an old philosophical problem that asks, whether the contents of a room still exist if there is noone there to observe them. The answer to this is, yes, of course the objects in the room are still there because consciousness is not confined to an observing individual but is present at all times everywhere. Once you accept that Brahman is not only everywhere but is also everywhere, then the philosophers' problem about non-observance goes away.

We have to get away from our common perception that there is a universe out there being separately observed by us. The only reality is Brahman consciousness and *we* (who are it) observe, as it were, from the inside out.

Our problem at all times is the limitations in our own atman incarnations in matter. In our human form we do not witness a complete reality. For a start, we have to make special instruments to detect forces we cannot see like x-rays and radio waves. But we also cannot see the big picture as Brahman in its fullness does and can only guess at what we are missing. In deep meditation the Oneness of Brahman can be glimpsed to a greater or lesser extent but it has never been described. We have to accept that all material things can only be fully described in relation to the Whole and that no thing has any reality on its own.

Advaita philosophy makes copious use of metaphors to illustrate its arguments. Perhaps the one I like most is to compare physical reality to the waves on the top of an ocean where the ocean beneath is the true Brahman reality. The waves come and go and ultimately have no independent existence, but the sea of consciousness beneath is the true reality.

The trouble with most Advaitin metaphors is that they never can go far enough, limited as they must be by language. This is true even of the ocean and wave metaphor. I would suggest that our physical world is more than a ripple on the surface of Brahman but is a very large part of the deeps itself.

Whereas at the centre of Brahman is the Godhead much (perhaps most) is hard-wired into its maya creation of the physical world. After all, that is the choice God has made – to experience itself more completely through incarnation (Brahman) into a material creation. This is the leap into the non-dual paradigm of understanding that we have to make. God's consciousness is the sole reality and it exists throughout and within the material realm which itself it has created.

Once you accept the unitive state it becomes possible to address the scientists' problem of how the observer affects the observed. The observer affects the observed because they are one and the same and the observer (Brahman) is ultimately the creator (or determiner) of what is being observed. The indeterminate reality at the quantum level that the scientists observe should be the prompt to inform us that there is no fixed materiality other than what we ourselves determine.

Our difficulty in understanding this is really one of scale. We live in the big, macro world that is the aggregated sum of countless quantum states and witnessed as though it were a generalisation. The physicist will insist there is a difference between our top-down consciousness and whatever is the force that links two quantum particles at a distance. But there lies the mistake. Our consciousness and the "mysterious" consciousness between two quantum particles is the same one Brahman consciousness.

We could possibly conclude that the association between particles at the quantum level is the absolute elemental manifestation of Brahman and that our own conscious experience is just a kind of "bigged up" version of that. Scientists are right to look for the ultimate nature of reality at the quantum level but they are still puzzled by the different rules that apply to that world compared to the macro world in which we live. Einstein was still looking for the answer on his deathbed.

Until science embraces the idea that both macro and micro reality is embraced within an underlying consciousness that we call Brahman, they will continue to be looking for the wrong thing.

ψ

Will science ever be able to "detect" or "measure" Brahman? I have always believed that, one day, science and religion will come together and form a complete, holistic view of reality and that would, indeed, be the start of a New Age. The Upanishads tell us that Brahman is without any quality whatsoever and that it is essentially unknowable in human terms. I don't think that should put off scientists who know all about testing a hypothesis. Physicists often assume the existence of such-and-such particle or force without having evidence that it is actually there. The current quest for the so-called Higgs Boson particle is just such a quest for something that it has been assumed "must be there".

The difference with Brahman, however, is that there is no known way of testing for it whereas with the Higgs Boson we know that if you build a particle accelerator big enough you will certainly find it if it is there. You can sense, however, that scientists are becoming braver as frustration grows with the conviction that something is missing. What is needed is a marriage of scientific hypothesising and philosophic logic. Science seeks the source of consciousness and examines the human brain to find how our awareness is wired.

But philosophy will ask awkward questions which science evades. We say, for example that the eye "sees" by focusing photons of light on the retina which then sends a signal via the optic nerve to the brain which reconstructs the electrical inputs as a picture. But what sees that picture? Even if you suggest some brain process, after that you are still left with the question of what sees that? You cannot philosophically argue for the existence of consciousness without accepting that consciousness is not constructed by the nervous system but is actually a primal state, an underlying film of awareness that permeates every-thing. Our brains cannot "see" on their own. Every sentient experience is only truly witnessed on the giant cinema screen that is Brahman.

Consciousness studies are well established in the academic world these days and there is openness in discussing the exact nature of our own awareness. If only the researchers would address the philosophical problem of "what sees that" we might arrive at a hypothesis that there exists an underlying ground consciousness onto which every sense input is reflected or witnessed. That, of course, is Brahman.

Could such a hypothesis be tested? Perhaps, but I rather doubt Brahman realisation amongst humanity will be a product of conventional scientific research. Unlike the background radiation said to have proved the Big Bang theory Brahman will not be detected as a hiss picked up by a radio telescope. Nor, I suspect, will it be inferred as a result of the high-speed collisions in a particle accelerator. Brahman may eventually be acknowledged as a kind of untestable theory by a future generation of physicists but it is essentially beyond description as the sages have always told us.

And, of course, it should be beyond description. Brahman is God's consciousness "projected as evolutionary energy" and thus the Absolute, the infinite dynamic that is unknowable even unto itself.

David Bohm, however, in his book "Wholeness and the Implicate Order", suggests that this "hidden variable" which lies behind the universe may, indeed, one day be measurable. Bohm has speculated that the universe might exist as some sort of hologram in which the real reality is an "implicate order" wherein each part of the creation somehow contains the sum of its parts.

Bohm has written that what we call empty space is actually an as yet undiscovered sea of energy, "and that matter as we know it is a small, 'quantized' wavelike excitation on top of this background, rather like a tiny ripple on a vast sea." Bohm continues, "….. what we perceive through the senses as empty space is actually the plenum, which is the ground for the existence of everything, including ourselves."

Bohm is a respected physicist but his speculations are a very good example of modern science coming to see reality in terms very similar to how the composers of the Upanishads taught us about Brahman.

Bohm did not call his "ground for the existence of everything" Brahman but he may as well have done. Perhaps Bohm's idea of an implicate order is a good way of imagining the way Brahman creates the material world through Maya? Could Maya actually be an implicate order enfolded within Brahman? In other words Brahman is "charged" with an implicate order that acts as the design instructions for creation. Brahman's implicate order works as a kind of hologram which projects the same programme in all parts of the universe. That programme is to order matter into ever more conscious forms because it is a projection or "development" of consciousness itself.

Our problem with this sort of speculation about the nature of physical reality is always one of being unable to picture what we are saying. We have to accept that we are, in a sense, locked into seeing one layer of reality that provides us with a focus too narrow to witness the fullness of the universe. We want to see as God sees but we wear blinkers and are forced into abstractions in order to see into what we cannot see.

We can speculate, for example, that there may be no material existence at all and that all that really exists is energy (for which read Brahman) that becomes matter only as a consequence of collapsed wave fronts. Put another way, we may say that matter is a kind of *perceived* condensate of the true wave energy of Brahman. We see the wave energy as discrete bits of matter only because we lack knowledge of the whole. If we knew the whole, everything would appear to be One, to be interconnected and without duality.

Physicists since Einstein have been speculating in this direction even if there is still no consensus. But you try and picture this unitary wave nature of reality! The world we witness seems very solid and we can hack at it, saw it, chop it up and feel it in all its obvious solidity. To be told that matter is just a collapsed wave front hardly seems helpful and flies in the face of our common sense.

This is the point where the (scientic or spiritual) seeker must realise that without reconditioning the mind there is no possibility that heightened consciousness can be achieved. Unless you become adept at seeing the world from a different perspective, from being able to cast off the blinkers, then grasping the strangeness of the universe is always beyond your reach. And this is exactly what higher religious instruction has always aimed to do.

Buddhist masters have been known to beat their disciples with a stick in order to stop them thinking along our normal pathways. That is why Hinduism urges long courses of studying under a guru or why Christian mystics sat for days on top of columns or retreated to the desert. It is why Sufis enter trance-like states, performing whirling dances, or why shamans perform exotic rituals and sometimes shock the mind through use of hallucinogenic materials.

You cannot just say "I am Brahman" and hope to take your consciousness to a higher vantage point. Only through practicing methodical religious instruction of whatever creed will you be able to alter your mindset sufficiently to see beyond. That is why we have religions.

$$\psi$$

One of the greatest challenges facing any religion is how it accommodates itself with the modern evolutionary theory of life. That religions continue to run up against Darwin's theory of Natural Selection as though it was some alternative belief system is a great pity. Evolution of some sort is an undeniable fact unless those fossils in ancient rock strata have been put there to fool us by a god with a sense of humour! Many people of faith have come to accept the slow evolution of life on this planet without needing to be any less devout but it is striking how many others cannot reconcile a creative God with an evolving universe.

Fewer still have come into contact with what is now called process theology wherein it is postulated that God itself is not some static changeless entity but is actually evolving along with all creation. But even those, like myself, who are happy to see religion and science as two sides of the same search for truth can have problems actually picturing why a purposeful God *chose* the randomness of the evolutionary process to bring about life.

When we ask, "why is the universe the way it is?" then perhaps we are posing the wrong question. Scientists say that they could postulate a universe with different laws to the one we see and that if there is a god then the existing laws must have been chosen for a reason. But scientists have not created the universe and perhaps the truth is that there is no other way for the universe to be than the way it appears?

"That thou art," advaitins like to say. This is where it is necessary to grasp the very "now-ness" of advaita, its almost existential way of saying that what is before you is the truth and you have nowhere further to look. The universe is the way that it is because there is no other way it could appear. The universe *is* God. All that ever exists is God's consciousness projected as evolutionary energy through Brahman. The universe is God's experience as a whole and we are fragments of that experience.

Consciousness slowly evolves in the universe because the universe itself is a conscious projection, a screen of awareness that reflects its own image onto matter. Our mistake is always the mind/matter duality where we make a distinction between conscious forms and inanimate matter. There is no such distinction. Consciousness is only a matter of degree and every-thing should be seen as having the characteristics of awareness.

Two atoms colliding make an impact on the conscious substratum of the universe. In the case of a human being, its fantastic complexity and heightened consciousness is only a scaling up of awareness at the microscopic level. Indeed, without understanding quantum consciousness we will not understand the nature of our own consciousness. The scaling up of consciousness into the life forms we recognise, is the inevitable product of the momentum of Brahman towards greater and greater ordering. Over time the oneness of Brahman exerts its unitive quality through interconnectedness, by ordering matter into complex forms that ultimately becomes conscious of themselves.

If you are still having difficulty picturing this then recall that quantum science has already shown that particles can "stay in touch" with each other over a distance and also that particles have no individual reality without reference to the whole. The universe is already whole even before evolution starts to take place. Life forms are building on a implicate complexity which is there already.

It seems as though, in the right conditions, the underlying interconnectedness of everything takes over and life forms "know themselves" into existence. In quiet planetary backwaters where the chemical soup of creation is able to form complex molecules, the innate instinct of matter to be conscious causes the bonding that will ultimately result in simple cellular life. The force that creates life does not come from outside but from within. The imperative within creation is to be conscious and to become more conscious still. We constantly go astray when we have a top-down view of nature, when it is only possible to understand when we look from the bottom-up, from the quantum level to our everyday level. Bohm must have been along the right lines when he imagined an implicate order contained in every particle of creation. But to imagine this implicate order you have to get the emphasis right and never lose sight of Brahman.

The implicate order is that all is interconnected and that nothing has any reality without reference to the One. With this oneness comes about the possibility of creation and the possibility of wonderful things.

If we are still having difficulty picturing this oneness of the universe then we might move on to visualising a universe in which there is no matter at all but only waves. Science has already gone down this route but has been averse to recognising the philosophical implications of its theorising. Let us imagine that Brahman is actually a form of wave energy, a broadcast of consciousness from God. Only don't visualise this like some form of long frequency wavelength like a radio wave but as a super-high frequency presence which issues from every direction and is present everywhere at once. This is the one Brahman presence and the extended consciousness of God. Where these Brahman waves collide the wave collapses to form a sub-atomic particle, the stuff out of which creation will evolve. The particle is simply a product of wave energy and has no independence or identity without its context as a product of a larger wave-based reality. This is another way of saying what the ancient Hindu holy men have always said about Brahman creating the world through Maya. They did not know what Maya was but we can speculate that it is no more than the process of Brahman wave energy breaking down to form matter. From Brahman consciousness comes matter. The first principle of reality is conscious awareness, that self-reflectedness in the void that is God. Out of this awareness comes what we witness as the creation but it is never anything less than that awareness itself.

The convertibility between matter and energy is a well-known scientific truth and Einstein's equation $E=mc2$ tells us of the enormous power locked up in every particle. But we now have to consider that all matter is ultimately convertible back into Brahman. Matter ultimately can convert back into the energy field of consciousness that is Brahman. But how do we do that? If I burn wood it converts into heat and light energy, not into Brahman.

Our inability to convert matter into its ultimate state of Brahman is because of our ignorance about Brahman in the first place. If we had the insight of an adept, of a Christ or a Sai Baba, we would understand how we can interact with fundamental reality and use our willpower to shape or mould aspects of physical existence.

It is all about knowing that you are the wave of Brahman, that you are enormously more important than you thought and that if you knew how the wave interacts with the power of superimposition which is Maya then great power would be yours.

There is a profound verse in the Tao Te Ching that shows this principle of interchangability between Brahman and Maya (or Tao and Te) has been gleaned before:

"He who knows the play of Tao and Te
knows the nature of the universe
Tao brings forth Te from its own being
Te expands in all directions
filling every corner of the world
becoming the splendour of all creation
Yet at every moment Te seeks Tao
This is the movement that guides the universe
This is the impulse
that leads all things back home.

Tao Te Ching, verse 65

To begin to understand how Brahman *works* we will have to turn our mental conditioning inside out. Today, most of us do not know the play of Tao and Te but it is nothing less than what science is really looking for. It is the interplay between consciousness and what we witness as the material world. To get there we will need to see the universe from the inside out.

Humankind has always looked upon the universe as consisting of empty space with matter being the stuff of creation and which occupies that space. We insist that matter is particulate in nature and that all reality consists of separate *things*. We have got things the wrong way round. Reality is actually the empty space not the things that seem to exist within it. What we think of as the void is the ground of Being and is not empty but full of the energy of Brahman. This is truly hard to imagine but that is because our consciousness is limited, we lack knowledge of the whole and ordinarily remain trapped into a material way of seeing things.

I have tried to make an approach to Brahman using the theorising of contemporary science. This is not to say that Advaitins or any those of any religious persuasion need resort to science in order to underpin their beliefs. But a world in which we have scientific truth and religious truth mutually exclusive of each other seems absurd. There is only one Truth but many pathways that lead towards it. The meeting point between religion and science is probably the perception of beauty because even scientists admit that they are often attracted to a theory because of its inherent aesthetics. In The Emperor's New Mind Penrose talks of scientific ideas that ring true and of rigorous argument actually being the last phase of scientific enquiry. It is with ideas that "ring true" that religion has always been concerned.

ψ

Vedanta for a New Age

Is India a better place for all its celebrated religious insight? If India has been the font of such wisdom why has this not shaped the nation into something distinctively correct and harmonious? The India we see today is so variegated, complex and often chaotic that nowhere do we see the stamp of a profound underlying philosophy or some guiding principle. India has been no stranger to wars, corruption, poverty and materialism and its faiths no less subject to sectarianism, fanaticism and bigotry. If Vedanta is the truth, then shouldn't we expect to see something different in India?

The veracity of Vedanta and its relevance to the modern world is a huge question that needs to be addressed particularly at a time when the world is crying out for change. We should also be mindful of how in the West those who have flirted with Advaita Vedanta have often tired of the idea as they find it leads nowhere and fails to inform us how to act. So what use is it all? What good does Brahman realisation do for an individual? You could easily say that those few who have entered into a fully realised Brahman state of consciousness have hardly changed the world. The many of us who intellectually grasp Brahman but never achieve the full unitive state of spirituality achieved by the gurus and swamis and "holy men" could also be questioned for what benefit it does us or anyone else? We still have to live in the world, we have to work, pay our taxes and bring up families. It's fine for India's saints to experience samadhi every day when they are supported by donations from their followers and they don't have to battle with the every day life of the rest us. Has all the philosophical speculation and spiritual experience of India done the world one jot of good?

The first thing to say about these questions is that very few people have ever achieved any deep knowledge or experience of

77

Brahman. In the West many of us have acknowledged Brahman at an intellectual level but have neither the willpower nor commitment to follow the tough spiritual path that leads to full realisation. In India, most Hindus get no further than a genuine reverence for their gurus or swamis and their spirituality stops at temple ritual. Most of us just don't get very far. Those who followed the hippy trail to Haridwar and Risikesh in the end came back with bits and pieces of Indian wisdom but then blended it in with a hotchpotch of New Age ideas. The idea that you might need to use self-discipline and change your behaviour to achieve spiritual insight never really caught on in an age of self-indulgent pleasure seeking. In truth, Advaita Vedanta has not had much of a chance yet.

Just because the concept of non-duality and Brahman is an ancient one does not mean that it is widely understood. Does the average Christian know much about the Old Testament? Often the time has to be right for an idea and the time for Advaita is perhaps only just arriving.

We also suffer from a lack of perspective. Our mortal lifetimes are too short for us to add up and witness the true contribution of the experiences of each and every one of us. We are part of a vast big picture and our perspective of the timespan over which the universe is unfolding is incomprehensible relative to human longevity. It is yet early days. The human species took five million years to evolve from the level of the apes and before that it took three billion years for life to proceed from the amoeba to primate. Who are we to get impatient with progress? From what we know it has only been in the last three or four thousand years that mankind has deeply explored its spiritual context and the insight of the Brahman reality been gained. Even then it is a fraction of mankind who have even dwelt upon the Brahman reality and an even smaller fraction who have achieved moksha. So it really is early days. The fact that during the last 100 years the knowledge of Brahman has spread outside of India and has attracted seekers in the West shows that Advaita Vedanta is yet young and not only needs to be heard by more people but can also be developed and refined by the new adherents.

All very well, you say, knowing that all is evolving over the millennia, but I live in a timeframe of less than 100 years and I want results today.

As soon as you pose this question you show your lack of knowledge of Brahman. The God consciousness which is Brahman does not exist in time. Once you know Brahman, time ceases to have real meaning and the question you are asking drops away. Your sense of Brahman is complete in itself, a moment of infinite bliss which is a feedback within the timeless Brahman consciousness of the universe. You are Brahman contemplating itself and all is closed within the perfect circle of awareness. True Advaitins lose all sense of angst, impatience and unease about life because they know that all you ever can seek in life is here in this very instant. There is nothing worth seeking other than the total perfection of the present moment. Brahman is eternal and timeless and within its embrace everything is held in perfection. This does not mean that you don't go out to work, study for a degree or fail to act in the world. We all have our individual yogas to perform. But what changes for an Advaitin is a change in conscious outlook, an ability to live for the present and not to worry unduly about the future. Jesus, too, taught the importance of living in the present:

"Can anxious thought add a single day to your life?"

Matt 6,27

"So do not be anxious about tomorrow; tomorrow will look after itself."

Matt 6,34

How can we not worry about the future, you ask? Surely, we have to plan, make strategies, save money or arrange travel plans? That is not what we mean about living in the Now. When you live intensely in the Now what happens is a change in your consciousness where your mind-centred, time-based consciousness drops away and is replaced by your true atman, soul-based consciousness. This is Brahman realisation and it is a spiritual power with which we can change the world.

Eckhart Tolle explained the importance of this focus on the present in his book The Power of Now and has no doubts about the importance of the spiritual power that can be released.

"If the Earth is to survive, this will be the energy of those who inhabit it."

Eckhart Tolle, The Power of Now

What is wrong with the world is our state of consciousness. Not only do we wrongly identify our consciousness as our minds but also we are so obsessed with time that we never live fully in the present. The ultimate way of living intensely in the present is to meditate and you can achieve this in ordinary waking life quite easily. Just try it. Try focusing your attention on this absolute split second and walk around with nothing else on your mind other than enjoyment of the instant. You will be surprised how changed you will feel. You will feel content, perhaps blissful, and you will even sense a sort of power. Imagine if everyone went around like that!

When we ask what good does Vedanta do, we can perhaps see what good it *could* do. If we lost our obsession with time and achieve contentment through focus on the present, all unnecessary desires, all greed and evil intent will fall away. We will be happy with our lot and cease to put demands on the world that are unsustainable. It is only by changing our whole mental outlook that we can change the world and that truly would be a New Age.

ψ

There is a movement today amongst some spiritual thinkers which wants to create a kind of critical mass of enlightened souls which, when achieved, would effectively trip mankind *en mass* into a new state of consciousness. Through group meditation or the passing of a blessing on ever-larger numbers of people it is felt that we have the ability to achieve a kind of collective super-consciousness. The number of people needed to form this oneness in consciousness is surprisingly small relative to the global population. One million souls, perhaps, would probably be enough to create a sway that would reverberate through the whole world.

This concept of shared consciousness is very similar to the line of thinking made popular by Rupert Sheldrake that argues learnt behaviour amongst part of a species is often transmitted though a kind of species or "morphic field" to the rest of the population. Given the speed with which information is transmitted today there already clearly exists the physical network to broadcast any new development to a global population. The powerful media of film, television and the internet can create a universal awareness of new developments in very short spaces of time.

Global brands are just one obvious manifestation of how trans-national awareness can easily be established if the idea or concept is right. But this is not quite what the movers behind this critical mass of souls idea have in mind. The unity that is required should not be based on communicating through the mass media but rather by sharing our Brahman consciousness and recognising its oneness.

The inherent difficulty in trying to achieve this unitary consciousness is that each one of us is a unique filter of experience and we bring to the group our different karmas, priorities, biases and experience. The individuality of experience is why the religious history of mankind is so diverse and constantly subject to new emphasis or insight. To make us all resonate to the same wavelength is asking a lot.

The congregational or collective form of prayer has a long history in most religions but that has not prevented a myriad of cults, divisions and different interpretations. The power of collective prayer should be a real phenomenon but how often does it work? The long list of requests made in the prayers of intercession in a Christian church makes an ambitious demand on each member of the congregation to focus fully on every appeal. And that is the heart of the problem. Prayer works when we get it right within ourselves. You can assemble as many souls as you like and it will not create any force whatsoever unless the focus, concentration and witness are razor sharp. In theory, the collective experience of Brahman should work for the obvious reason that we are all part of the One. In practice, it can be questioned whether the congregational practice finds what it sets out to seek.

Christ seemed quite dismissive of public worship and told his disciples it was better to go in to a darkened room and on their own and pray to the Father. Christ never even set out to found a new religion but stressed the simple message of forgetting yourself, living in a spirit of love and giving, and worshipping God. You won't find any of the Indian spiritual masters setting up any religions of their own, any movements or cults. Instead, the Indian way is for the enlightened soul to set up an ashram and let seekers come to them for guidance. Hinduism is not a prose-lytising religion but rather a pathway littered with signposts. Similarly, the Buddha only asked others to try his path for themselves and never thought in terms of "Buddhism".

The Western approach has tended to be more systematic and to reduce spiritual witness to structured creeds, churches and organisations. It is a cultural disposition of the Western mind to want to order and control, to package everything up so that it can be sold like a commodity. This, I fear, is what is happening in parts of the New Age movement where the instinct is for pulling people together and trying to forge the same mind-set. I distrust movements of any kind because as soon as you join one, something is lost. There is only ever the individual seeking the truth and we would not be created as the indwelling atman soul if it were not the intention that our paths would be singular. Movements always have leaders and leaders always want to impress their thoughts on others.

The spiritual masters have always told us that you must be discerning in matters of religion – as soon as you start accepting somebody's else's version of reality you run the risk of getting it wrong. This is why it must be a lone quest. You must constantly question what you hear, compare, analyse and synthesise. You can only do this on your own although, of course, you pull in other people's experience along the way. Distrust movements of any kind. As soon as you join one you will find it has its own politics and annoying people who want to be in control. Trust in your own search and accept that it will be lonely. Be open and prepared to listen and never doubt that many you listen to have fallen from the razor thin path. There are many amongst the New Agers who have got it wrong. You can usually tell them by their dress or eccentric behaviour or their tendency to believe in anything going rather than be discriminating.

A good cure for the modern tendency towards gullibility is to read John Bunyan's 17th century spiritual classic "The Pilgrim's Progress", which spelt out quite bluntly how easy it was to get it wrong along the way:

"Look before thee; dost thou see this narrow way? That is the way thou must go. It was cast by the Patriarchs, Prophets, Christ, and his Apostles, and it is as straight as a Rule can make it: This is the way thou must go."

John Bunyan, Pilgrim's Progress

The Indian masters of Vedanta philosophy would agree with Bunyan that the path is narrow, razor thin, and that it is important to discriminate and persist on the lone quest to get it right. Bunyan may have known nothing about other religions but he would no doubt be able to recognise the difference between a lunatic and a genuine holy man or woman. He would have known that the spiritual path requires humility and discipline, that you need a teacher or a guru, that you need to follow the wisdom teachings that have stood the test of the ages, and that as soon as you go off on a tangent you will likely get it wrong. Read the spiritual classics, the gospels, the Koran, the Upanishads and the writings of the mystics. Distrust those who want to condemn and punish. As soon as you hear fundamentalist rantings, bigotry and intolerance, you are hearing those who have got it wrong. Those who will not except scientific knowledge and cannot reconcile it with their religion have got it wrong. Be a big spirit and brave enough to recognise that you don't know everything but that you are here to explore.

ψ

There is a widespread belief amongst New Age thinkers that mankind is about to make a massive evolutionary leap, which will involve a shift to a higher state of consciousness. Today this belief is almost always tied up with the prediction, originally drawn from the Long Count in the Mayan calendar, that a great change will take place in the year 2012. The literature and web-based material available on the 2012 theory has become so enormous that it easy to become baffled at the many takes on the subject which include Galactic Alignments, the discovery of ancient Egyptian libraries, geomagnetic reversals, comet impacts, the appearance of a new planet and biochemical changes in our brains. There is no doubt a lot of wishful thinking in many 2012 theories and as a phenomenon in itself, 2012 says much about mankind's anxious state of mind at the moment.

The expectation that mankind is heading for some massive defining event is growing and is not hard to see why. Even if we forget what ancient calendars seem to be telling us, that we are pointing to a culmination of our era in some way, we all know by now that we are living in an unsustainable oil-based economy with a financial system that is driven by nothing less than insatiable greed, that the pressure on resources is rising as the population explodes, and that our pollution of the Earth is in danger of destroying the environment. 2012 may or not be a date with destiny but the howling need to re-order the politico-economic world picture is surely the siren voice of the age . The signs are there already as the world powers muscle themselves into position to grab world resources. Add to this an intense feeling of moral crisis as a divide opens between fundamentalist faith-based views of humanity's purpose and rampant consumerism, and there is a powder keg waiting to blow. This is why so much angst and expectation is building up around the 2012 date. It simply seems highly probable that something must change – and soon.

Personally, I do not think that there is any need to attach significance to the 2012 date itself. It stretches my credulity too far to believe that ancient cultures had the ability to see precise events in the distant future and that everything is so pre-determined that we are essentially running on automatic.

Human destiny has always been influenced by chance events and who knows what flapping of the butterfly's wings will tip us one way or another in the future. I suggest that the focus on the 2012 date may serve another purpose and that is to push our own destiny in a way we choose rather than wait for disasters from outer space.

We are all one – Brahman – so significant changes of behaviour or thought can be communicated across a species as a kind of holistic awareness. Think of how the world religions like

Christianity, Islam, and Buddhism caught on like wildfire in their early stages. Today, this ability for rapid paradigm change is even facilitated further by global communication marvels like the internet. Changes in thinking and spiritual awareness no longer need be isolated for long with individuals but can be transmitted instantly to millions around the globe. But what is the big idea that is going to change everything and bring in the New Age?

Take a step back for a moment and consider human evolution. Have you ever really dwelt on how truly awesome is the human story? When I studied human evolution at university I was always left with the nagging feeling that something was missing. I was left feeling amazed at how quickly the hominid line developed with the human brain tripling in cranial capacity over that of our nearest relatives the chimpanzees in just 5 million years. In evolutionary time that is nothing. Was something speeding up the rate of our own evolution? There is new evidence that the rate of mutation of the human genome has indeed speeded up over time but that in itself is not evolution. There has to be selective pressure on these mutations for evolution to take place and personally I cannot see enough of this pressure to believe that it can create the difference between ape and man in just 5 million years.

So is there some kind of evolutionary feedback mechanism in place where because of Brahman and our absolute conscious inter-connectedness, we ultimately pull ourselves up by our own bootstraps? Is it possible that Brahman creates its own momentum towards higher consciousness and is actually its own super-selective mechanism, pre-disposing man for mutations which create greater intelligence / awareness / self-reflection? In other words, we are not just the chance result of environmental selective pressures but also the most stunning result of a universal imperative towards higher consciousness.

Once you acknowledge Brahman you will be drawn inevitably to ask how does this underlying consciousness impact the process of natural selection? All that evolves is Brahman anyway; just a projection of its own consciousness, so is Brahman *shaping* evolution towards some end? If Brahman's evolutionary imperative is towards higher life forms, why was it that on the Earth we had to create so many evolutionary paths, including dead-ends, before we get to human?

You could say that Brahman might as well get to human in one bound rather than go through billions of years of random mutations. Consider, however, that Brahman does not interact with natural selection but that it is a latent power that advances once life forms achieve a certain level of consciousness.

Clearly, as evolutionary energy, Brahman at first creates the evolving universe with conditions right for the emergence of life under the rules of natural selection. From then on there is no need to interfere. It is simply logical that higher consciousness will emerge because in the end intelligence is the most adaptive of all pathways which life can go down and sooner or later it will always win out. When that higher intelligence emerges, as it does in humankind, then the impetus of Brahman starts to hold sway and tilts evolution towards higher consciousness. It is like a feedback mechanism where the product of Brahman recognises its creator and uses its power to further develop its intelligence. Consider, too, that it was this feedback mechanism that was taking place in some subtle way during human evolution.

As mutations led to greater brain capacity and complexity there was an increase in Man's powers of self-reflection and moments when individuals touched upon something interfused in nature which held them in awe. As soon as Brahman begins to be recognised, its powers are stirred and a potential is awoken. Did Brahman lend a momentum to human evolution that focused on increasing brain power and increasing conscious awareness? It is difficult to picture because it calls for some hidden interconnectedness between groups of hominids with perhaps a sharing of learned behaviour through a "field" of some sort. But it is interesting that this is exactly what some groups of the New Age are proposing with their group consciousness work. We may be about to discover what it was that pulled us up as an animal and realise that during our "civilised" years, we as a species have forgotten something incredible.

If we are about to go through some great change in our consciousness, in what direction should it go? This question is much easier to answer because not only do the great pandits of Brahman all agree but also the crisis of the modern world is crying out for the change. All our problems which beset us are because we are never happy with our lot. We always want more; we are always looking to the future for us to have more wealth, more expensive holidays, better cars and more consumer goods. So greedy are we that we are prepared to mortgage our children's' future just so that we can have today what we cannot yet afford. The financial crash is showing the utter lunacy of the way we have been living and that we need not just a new economic model but a complete change in our own conscious outlook.

Knowers of Brahman will agree that our object on Earth is to live in the present and to stop worrying about what we may or may not have in the future. Be satisfied with what you have, live in the moment and the future will take care of itself. Our whole financial market system is rigged on a gamble with the future rather than reflecting present value.

We must lower our sights and change our sense of value so that we price what someone gives and not what they take. People should work so that they can give, selflessly to others. Value giving, not taking. The pandits tell us we should live lightly going through life without asking for anything but always wanting to do for others, and live with compassion and love. This is the change that must come about and it will require a complete revolution in our minds for it to be achieved.

It is almost axiomatic amongst New Agers that this change can be brought about if enough people get together and will the change. Whether it happens like this is uncertain. The important thing is to recognise the power of Brahman and that it is there waiting for us to call it into action. Those who have used the power of Brahman have tended to use it sparingly and often in relative secrecy. But first know Brahman and to know Brahman you must act. Only persistent spiritual exercise will lead you to Brahman and this requires action. You can't put the cart before the horse and try to use the power of Brahman before you have realised the One.

There are those who say that the Advaitin need do nothing but exist in contentment with their wisdom. This is wrong. You must act. One of the misunderstandings of Indian philosophy is that it is nihilistic and simply advocates a kind of dropout from life as you rest with a Brahman-inspired detachment. That would be meaningless. If our sole goal was to achieve Brahman awareness, discovery of the Self, then why have human life and why be here at all? We are God discovering itself through presence in a material, evolving universe and all the pain and happiness, strife, searching and experience is the experiment God has chosen to realise itself to the fullest. So live your life. Work in your own area, think, study, interact with as many people as possible, experience as much as you can, travel, explore, read, feel the very raw thrill of being alive. Whatever you do or experience is God experiencing itself for you are of God – a tiny fragment of its cosmic consciousness.

Many people take the religious path in search of some kind of "peace". People want a palliative, a cure or distraction from life's pains. There is no such thing. Live the pain, suffer and be agonised by life's torment. Only through pain can God experience itself to the fullest and the visceral experience of our own lives' feeds its ever-evolving sense of reality.

The universe is nothing other than a self-discovering

conscious process of which you are a part. Know that you are part of this cosmic experience. It is a tremendously empowering and inspiring idea when you fully realise how your life fits into the big picture. Sometimes our lives can seem full of trivia and annoyances and our self-esteem disappears. But every living, conscious creature is important because God is experiencing itself through them and that means you too.

Live your life as though you are God on a path of discovery because that is what God is doing – exploring a perhaps infinite world of experience so that God consciousness, or Brahman, can have more than itself to be conscious of.

ψ

Glimpses of Brahman

Aham brahmasmi. "I am Brahman". There is no higher under-standing, nowhere else to go after you say this – after you fully realise it. To know that you are Brahman is the ultimate goal of the Atman consciousness. It is life's end, the journey is over. Once the Atman consciousness realises it is Brahman and that the phenomenal world is simply Maya, a projection of Brahman, then Brahman has broken through, possessed your whole consciousness and filled you with the bliss and perfection of the ultimate indivisible reality. "That thou art".

Of course, the realisation of Brahman does not end your mortal life on earth, because the fully realised soul may still have work to do. Brahman brings selflessness, a oneness with all life and a compassion for other souls. Moreover, full self-realisation will automatically lead to a conviction that it must help other souls towards Brahman and to help build the reality of universal consciousness on earth. Brahman brings with it mission, charity and a determination to help others see through the veil of Maya and to the ground of the universe that lies behind our mortal experience.

Indian philosophy, as expressed by the Vedas, the Upanishads and Vedanta, today has earned a respect throughout the world which transcends all creeds and has even provided insight in modern science. It is not a single belief system but rather a number of philosophic strands to be explored but which all have their root in the concept that the many is an expression of the One.

There is no religion that cannot accommodate the sweeping vision of the Vedantic tradition. This is because the Hindu religion is a multi-faceted faith open to other belief systems and encourages a journeying, philosophic approach to spirituality. The Vedas asked for a questioning, trial-it-yourself and scientific approach for our soul journey. This non-dogmatic stance is what has made Indian religious thinking so attractive in the West and such a strong undercurrent in the New Age.

I am Brahman. Not just a mere phrase, not an abstraction but reality itself. To know that you are Brahman is to have brought your consciousness to its ultimate pitch here on Earth. Of course, anyone can say the words "I am Brahman". It is not the recitation of the words that is so important as to understand, at the very deepest level of your soul reality, that it is true. It is the intense, exhilarating and blissful inner awareness that comes with Brahman realisation that determines that you have reached your goal. To know Brahman is to have abandoned your body and mind, to have gone beyond sense awareness and thinking, to have merged your Atman with the reality of which it is a part. Your soul consciousness is the consciousness of the Universe, of God.

Mystics of all religions and throughout the ages have realised this. You can find this ecstatic state of conscious realisation every-where from the Sufi mystics to St Augustine, from Sai Baba to the day the Holy Spirit descended on Christ's Apostles. The individual can arrive at this understanding regardless of his or her starting point in time, race or culture. It is always the same thing, albeit described through the filter of the Atman's particular incarnation, whenever and wherever that may be.

"Whoever has ears to hear, let them hear". The pathways to God are many and the most important thing is just to get on with it. To understand who you are, your absolute reality, is life's goal. Self-discovery is our mission, our purpose. What use is wealth, worldly success or sense gratification when you are an incarnate soul that is part of God seeking its own realisation? Know this and live it and all the trivia, pain, and frustrations of human existence will become something to live lightly, to pass through as one observing your life from a lofty detachment.

Release your soul which is you. You are not your mind or your body. Those are perishable; the mere instruments, or eyes, of your conscious self. The ground consciousness of all space and time is the source of your true identity, the eternal, timeless expression of God. Don't waste time. Work and fulfil your duties on earth in a spirit of giving to others, of charity and service. But know that mortal works are no more than a testing ground for the soul.

The soul, or Atman, sees reality through its human filter, a distorting and limiting animal mechanism that can blind you of seeing the ultimate reality – if you let it. Break free from this bind because that is your test, that is why you are here. To express the conscious Brahman it needs to be challenged in material incarnations. Brahman (God) seeks its own perfection by self-realisation in the constricted consciousness of animal incarnation. That is what is happening inside you. God is struggling to get out, Brahman to shine through. How many have realised that all their inner searching, their frustrations, miseries and sense that "all is not right" is just that – for your true nature and identity to take hold and make sense of everything?

The crisis in the world today is not of a political, economic, social or environmental nature even though these issues are real enough. The problem for the human species is that we are falling short of our potential, our purpose and true evolutionary goal. Mankind has evolved to a state of awesome intelligence. It is this tool of intelligence that permits the Atman to achieve realisation of Brahman, to intuit its real identity and ultimately to free itself and return to and enrich the spirit of God. We are not God, but we are *of* God. When the spirit of God (which is Brahman) realises that it is *of* God then the cycle of self-realisation, of infinite consciousness, is turned once more and what is perfection becomes more perfect still.

"When I know what I am I discover that I am not existence,
I am the presence which allows existence to be"

Tony Parsons in The Open Secret

There is no boundary between Brahman and the Atman. All is one, Atman is part of Brahman. There is no duality between our personally realised consciousness and the total consciousness of Brahman. To talk of the Atman is only to use the verbal expressions of the mind to aid description. You are Brahman, a part of the whole and to fully realise your identity is to be empowered and set free.

Fully realised souls who have completed their cycle of rebirths in this world finally know the nature of reality and realise that the world of forms is only a projection of Brahman itself. This is Maya, the material expression of Brahman that we have talked about before. Brahman, by Maya, creates the world of forms through which it limits and tests itself so that it may be enriched and more fully realised. An earthbound soul which has realised its Brahman reality has a conscious understanding of Maya and is thus capable of miracles. The world of forms is determined by consciousness itself, by Brahman, and the individual Atman feels this and can (if it wants and chooses) perform the reality-changing miracles of a Jesus or Sai Baba.

Reality is only a construct of Brahman, of pure consciousness; thus, to realise Brahman is to be able to determine, or fix, reality. That is how miracles are performed. Miracles are reality-changing acts of Brahman consciousness.

All miracles are performed through conscious will. You cannot just say "I am Brahman" and perform miracles. It is the depth of your Brahman realisation that determines your power. To abandon self and feel the full reality of Brahman is hard and few ever make it. But there are those who have travelled the path and once they cross over into full realisation of Brahman they know, with a humble awareness, that power is now theirs.

Very few of us will ever experience the One with such intensity that we become miracle workers. Even though we might intellectually grasp Brahman that is very different from the complete surrender of ego, your sense of "I"-ness, that is required to experience the Ultimate. That is not to say that we should not try and that progress or "nearness" is not possible. Nor does that mean that we cannot experience brief fragments of perfect Brahman consciousness in those rare moments (often accidental) when we forget ourselves and see behind the veil. Many of us have these inexplicable moments but they are usually so breathtaking and exhilarating that we actually get scared and draw back behind the comforting sheaths by which Maya obscures us from Reality. In fact, why seek Brahman at all? If it is enough to intellectually grasp the concept why then not just get on with life that, after all, is all Brahman anyway? But Brahman is not something "out there", rather it is the here and now, it is the present moment and everything you are doing or sensing or thinking can never be anything less than Brahman whether you realise it or not.

We can "appreciate" Brahman even though few of us can achieve the complete abandonment of self that is required to realise our complete oneness with Brahman. The problem is that there is always an "I" experiencing something when in reality there is no "I" and no duality between the individual atman consciousness and the God consciousness of Brahman. But I do believe it is possible to make progress towards what we may call a lower form of enlightenment when even the intellectual grasp of Brahman brings us into the foothills of that ultimate bliss. Even if we do not achieve liberation from the sense that we are actually observing or experiencing something we can grasp without difficulty the truth that our consciousness is just a small part of a vastly bigger mirror. We are, of course, the mirror itself.

Within Advaita Vedanta itself there are different paths that are recommended depending on the nature of the individual.

You can choose, for example, the path of bhakti yoga that allows for the worship of a personal God as a way of realising Brahman consciousness. There is also karma yoga where adherents attempt to live their lives without incurring karma at all. You could easily be a Christian Advaitin and realise that the Holy Spirit is the same as Brahman and that Christ is the redeeming god through which you open up to Brahman. These paths are there for your own choosing but you can consider that you don't need a path at all.

The meaning of a path is that you are on a road to somewhere that lies ahead. You have not got there yet! But Advaita teaches that you are there already because there is at no moment any other truth than Brahman. All that exists is consciousness and you are no more than part of the play going on within that consciousness. Brahman exists whether you have got there on your path or not. Apart from the holy men who have renounced everything and sometimes appear almost mad is it not too much for most of us to expect to experience Brahman. Even in states of deep meditation (which itself is another "path") there is an inevitable "I" witnessing the calm and so the unitive state cannot be said to have been reached. This is the crux of our problem. If God's Brahman consciousness has created our Maya world with its obscuring sheaths so that we cannot see Reality why should we try and deconstruct. It is as though we are playing a game of hide-and-seek with God and what is the purpose of that?

Advaitin philosophy does not answer the question of why God created Reality as it did. The concept of Maya as the way the phenomenal world is some sort of projection of consciousness has never been properly developed and is difficult to grasp. But, as with any belief system, this is the leap of faith moment that is required if a higher level of understanding is to be achieved. This is the moment when you have to "believe" that what the holy men have told us over the ages is based on personal experience that is valid and not delusional.

The operative word is "experience". All religion is ultimately based on personal inner experience, those subtle shades of feeling which carry the conviction that something important has been sensed or felt. These personal experiences underlay the whole edifice of the Hindu religion just as much as they do in other faiths. These experiences must be respected because they represent our deepest intuitions about the nature of reality even if they so rarely lend themselves to words. In the case of Advaita the philosophy was not worked out with a pencil and a piece of paper but must derive from the gleanings of meditation and devotional practice. It comes from within and there is no way you can get away from this fact.

Most people reading this book will, I suspect, have had their own religious experiences somewhere during their lifetimes. Usually, these experiences are very fleeting and not at all frequent. These experiences will come in a variety of forms and, of course, will often be religion-specific if the person follows a particular faith. But I would strongly suggest that all religious experiences have the common element that they do not involve any sense of the ego/self but are instead concerned with a wider "flavour" or "feeling" about Reality. These flavours or feelings are always blissful; give a sense of wholeness and an exquisite glimpse of the moment abiding in its complete perfection. Words will never do it justice but we have to try.

There is with these experiences a feeling of the instant being suspended outside of time and bathed in a special light that is saying that everything is as it should be. It is a moment of affir-mation, a "fear not" feeling that your reality is special but part of a bigger picture which makes sense of everything. I may be wrong. Obviously, I can't know everyone's religious experiences. But I would chance that it is this loss of self – for an instant – which permits the experience. As we rid ourselves of our suffo-cating sense of a separate identity the greater Reality of Brahman subsumes us and, momentarily, we realise we are It.

"Anyone who wants to become a follower of mine
must renounce self".

Mk 8,34

Only a partial loss of the ego/self is needed for some sense of
Brahman consciousness to be acquired. Just a slight pulling back
of the veil will permit some light through. After all, people's
experiences of Brahman will come in different forms because
they are still filtering the experience through their own
individual spiritualities or religious choices. That shows that they
have not totally rid themselves of self but it is a start and, for
most of us, is as far as we will ever get. But take your cue from
these experiences. Take them seriously. Try and remember them
although it is nigh impossible to recall them at will.

If personal experience is to be your cue into Brahman then the
factor that will help multiply these experiences is *conviction*.
When we observe religious belief in a cold analytical way we can
be put off by the often fanatical way in which the belief is held.
But what may appear to be fanaticism is the result of deep inner
conviction, of a genuinely sensed "rightness" of direction. You
cannot make spiritual progress in a half-hearted manner. Only
with conviction can you achieve the inner change of heart, the
new perspective that is required to be a seer of Brahman.

In his wonderful book Understanding Islam, Frithjof Schuon
tried to describe to a Christian audience why the Muslim belief
that "God is One" becomes something greater depending on the
conviction with which it is held.

"...... what he [the Christian] cannot know straight away is
that all depends on the quality-on the sincerity (*ikhlas*)-of this
belief; what saves is the purity or the totality of the belief, and
that totality clearly implies the loss of self, whatever the form
in which this is expressed."

Frithjof Schuon in Understanding Islam

Critics might say that these deeply held religious convictions are a form of brainwashing yourself. Indeed, sometimes they are a form of brainwashing but beliefs are not the monopoly of the mentally well balanced and when the maladjusted adopt them these people are usually easy to spot.

Seekers of Brahman should expect that their growing insight would change them as individuals and even alienate you from some people. India's holy men are most often eccentric in some way and some have been quite controversial characters. This should not surprise us. To know Brahman is to experience a changed consciousness and you must expect that in some way you will be different. Losing your sense of self means that the things that preoccupy most people will have secondary importance to you and your attachment to the material world will diminish. You cannot know Brahman and ever be the same again.

ψ

Armed with our conviction, our determination to abandon the self and a hunger for experience the seeker of Brahman sets out on the journey. There is a lovely simile in the Upanishads where the seeker is likened to an arrow of devotion, the bow is the sacred scriptures and the bowstring is meditation. The Lord of love is the target.

"Now draw the bowstring of meditation
And hitting the target be one with him"
Mundaka Upanishad

So we pull the bowstring, let ourselves go and hit the target. Can that moment be described? It is surprising how little has ever been put into writing about the experiences which have been had by people in meditation even if achieving Oneness with Brahman is to go where description cannot follow.

One person brave enough to try and explain the experiences of meditation was Dr Paul Brunton who was one of those pioneering Western explorers of Eastern spirituality who appeared in the 20th century. Brunton was clear that all images or sensations experienced during meditation are not Brahman (which he called the Overself) but sometimes symbols of Brahman. These symbols can be acts of Grace where God provides encouraging hints of the Absolute and rendered to appeal to the individual through whatever cultural filter or religious predisposition is appropriate. To Brunton the meditator's experience of Brahman is "silent and scriptureless".

"What the student has to grasp is that where there is seemingly nothing at all but a static Silence, the Real abides; where his individual perception fails to register either form or entity, there the Overself IS."

Paul Brunton, The Wisdom of the Overself

In his groundbreaking book, A Search In Secret India, Brunton took a very discerning path towards his own enlightenment always looking to separate out the fraudulent from the genuine. His experience of Brahman, however, was crystal clear and his by now famous description of it about as convincing and precise as would be possible for such a numinous moment.

"I find myself outside the rim of world consciousness. The planet which has so far harboured me, disappears. I am in the midst of an ocean of blazing light. The latter, I feel rather than think, is the primeval stuff out of which worlds are created, the first state of matter. It stretches away into untellable infinite space, incredibly *alive*."

Paul Brunton, A Search In Secret India

Even in meditation the experience of Brahman can be very brief.

All the great sages confirm this and it seems that most of the time spent meditating is really spent *getting there*. The state of ecstasy called samadhi should also be seen as a form of precursor to the actual experience of Brahman. This is because there can be no emotion or anything relating to sentient human feeling at the moment of Brahman realisation because at that instant you ARE fully Brahman and no longer neither the separate Atman soul nor ego.

The last parting human feeling before we cross the bounds and into Brahman will be an intense feeling of love. This is because the soul is beginning to achieve a Oneness with the Universe and as we described in Chapter Two, Oneness is love. For many this feeling of a divine, all-embracing love will be like going into an ecstatic trance-like state which some of the great souls like Ramakrishna have been able to hold for long periods.

These experiences in the foothills of Brahman are important because for most of us it is where we will have nearly all of our religious experiences. Indeed, there are a number of ways to achieve inklings of Brahman which are no less impressive for being just symbols or elements of the Absolute. A good example of this would be the Christian practice of receiving Holy Communion. We can take the receiving of bread and wine as being merely symbolic of becoming one with Christ but any communicant will tell you that the grounding feeling and sense of cleansing which this practice induces is a very powerful religious experience. What matters always is the direction of the person's feelings, the intent behind the ritual. Again, it is like the arrow on the bowstring and what matters is that it is pointing at the target.

All the great spiritual teachers tell us that there are stages you must go through before you can attain the ultimate realisation of Brahman. Too many of us in the West have tried to get to the last stage first. Give your spiritual search time and be prepared to break off if you feel uncomfortable about it. Experience seems to show that devotional practice, which in Hinduism is called bhakti yoga, is one of the surest ways to base your quest upon something solid. Bhakti yoga combined with karma yoga, in which the seeker sees the significance of his or her life's actions, is probably as sound as you can make it.

If you think about it this is exactly the same as the central Christian practice of worship of God and attention to your moral course through life. Your ultimate attainment of Brahman realisation is a wholly different thing. In fact, strangely, you cannot achieve Brahman by actually seeking it. The strangeness is that you only experience Brahman by becoming IT – there can never be any question of an "I" witnessing Brahman. When you cast off the final sheath there will be no YOU seeing Brahman – only Brahman itself. This is why many of the great pandits tell us to pray or worship in a kind of disinterested way. Yes, the arrow of your intention must be aimed straight at your target, but you cannot climb up into Brahman but rather fall, almost accidentally, into it. As soon as you presume you know Brahman you have likely got it wrong. If your intention and practice has been correct, Brahman will eventually find you. And when Brahman does find you then the secret of creation will be revealed. This is the pinnacle moment when you can discern how Brahman brings the world of forms about through the process of Maya. It is the instant in which you see how Tao and Te interact, what Krishna meant by the union "the field" and "the knower of the field", the relationship between consciousness and matter wherein all miracles have their explanation. There is that finely balanced peak experience that is the end of the road for our spiritual search. To get there you will have to have done everything right; worked hard at it, sacrificed so much, been sincere in your quest, been patient rather than assuming and never dogmatic or deluded. It is the ultimate experience that awaits us all.

We need not ponder over long on those perfect Brahman moments but instead let us back track a little and search amongst those foothill occasions when we can come close to our goal, experience a glimpse of what lies beyond and gather ourselves before daring to go further. We shall now take flight and fire the arrow.

ψ

Call it "karmic shock". One of the surest ways to get close to Brahman realisation is to fully appreciate what karmic imprint you have made into it. When you truly know yourself in the karmic sense you are aware of the full impact you have made on the world around you and that you cannot get away from the fact that all our thoughts and actions are linked in a great karmic dance. It is not until you know your karma that you can go about trying to shake it off.

We all have those occasional moments when we see into ourselves and experience the quality or feel of our nature. When you do grasp the moment imagine yourself existing in a broad swathe of reality, as just a small cog in a giant wheel, a grain of sand on a vast beach. This is one of those perspective moments when things only make sense if seen as part of a bigger whole. Think of the whole universe as being made up of karma, of reaction and reaction, of cause and effect. Then see yourself as part of it and feel the thrill of Brahman, the elemental force from which everything has come.

You may have a lot of bad karma and feel burdened by it. This may be past life karma or a dark feeling that there is just something about you that is negative and can't be shaken off. To achieve moksha, liberation from the cycle of birth and death, all karma must be fully worked out or atoned. But there is no need to be worried or frightened about karma. Once you see your own karma in the round and realise that it is just part of the great karmic drama then it dwindles in significance.

In the anonymous medieval spiritual work The Cloud of

Unknowing the author likes to refer to his sin as something that exists in a filthy lump that stands between him and God. As long as you try to achieve this mental separation from your sin (or negative karma) and your intent is always on God then your karmic imprint is being lessened and your spiritual flight will gather speed.

ψ

See God in everything. If God is Brahman and Brahman is every-thing than God is present in everything. This is an axiomatic truth and it implies that God is reflected in all things. If you stop and contemplate this truth then the whole world seems to glow with a completeness that should take your breath away.

The Godness of everything should be your cue for spiritual progress. Man cannot achieve Oneness with the Godhead without trial and error, without effort and, most importantly, without assistance. Fortunately for man, there is a great deal of assistance available and it is all out there in the World because God is the World. You could, if you wished, worship God by worshipping a tree.

If contemplation of the tree "keyed" you into Brahman than there is no reason that cannot be your route to God. But just think how many are these routes to God. Christ came to mankind as a "route" to God, as a facilitator, an exemplar and spiritual assist. But there are many others. In Islam we have the prophet Mohammed as another man soul pointing the way to Paradise. In Hinduism there is Vishnu and Shiva existing like the polarities of God's nature to guide us into the centre. But there are still more. Within our outer reaches of Brahman exist knots of spiritual power that we may generally call angels but which I call collec-tively "fully realised souls". Call upon these spiritual helpers and prepare to be amazed at what happens.

Souls like my Sai Baba of Shirdi are tangibly near. They are too many to list but one with tremendous potency at the moment is the Archangel Michael. Tilt your soul towards such spirits, pray to them and ask for their assistance and you will almost feel as though you are literally taking flight.

Always be open to spiritual metaphors. Because God cannot be described or represented it is natural to find our own token way of depicting what we seek.

All faiths have found the need to symbolise or represent God in some way because we seek a physical focus for our spiritual search. The iconoclasts of world history have never been able to win out because it is just human nature to want to put form where there is no form, pattern where there is abstraction and something tangible when there is only mystery. Even in Islam, where to represent God in any image is seen as blasphemy, there is still the Koran itself to represent the Absolute, something physical and itself iconic and revered as the Word. As always, what matters is the depth of spiritual feeling and the sheer hunger of the longing for Truth, which validates the particular route you take.

"God is spirit, and those who worship him must worship in spirit and in truth."

Jn 4,24

ψ

Understand the Law of Attraction. It is really a karmic principle that whatever you tend to seek most you will, in the end, actually find. If you seek God, you will find God. The Law of Attraction is about predisposition, it is your angle of attack and compass heading. If you are interested in robbery you will sooner or later rob someone. Witnessing the Law of Attraction in action is a very spiritual experience.

The Law is a much wider phenomenon than that of simply

always receiving what you seek. It also shapes those particular times when you have a sudden experience of profound self-knowledge. Take those moments when you recognise yourself in another person. You and that other person exchange that glance of recognition that is truly astonishing. What is happening? At the very deepest level of the soul you and that other soul have some shared intuition, or previous life experience or common predisposition. This is a glimpse of Brahman because the feeling is of Oneness and Brahman is One. Two people together is a very powerful spiritual force. Christ told his disciples that whenever two or more of them prayed together they would get what they asked for.

"Whatever you pray for in faith, you will receive".
Matt 21,22

The Law of Attraction is a little understood spiritual principle that actually lies at the heart of much that we would usually call the paranormal. Just take it a little deeper and we can see why. We are Brahman, part of the creative ground awareness of the universe, and in a fragmentary way are able to wield the power TO BE.

If we tend towards some wish, some desire to bring something about we actually can because we exist within the creative energy field of Brahman. So to desire something is to unleash a latent power because in microcosm it is the same as the original desire of Brahman to create the universe. "Desire and creation" is the same as saying "cause and effect" and is the whole dynamic behind the karmic universe. If only man knew how much power he truly had we would not have to invent terms like Law of Attraction but realise there is only the Law of Brahman and that we are IT.

ψ

"The best use of this Moment is to drown in it." This instruction comes from the Indian poet and mystic Papaji who understood the here and now of Brahman. To concentrate solely on the present instant is, of course, at the heart of meditational practice. But you don't have to go into meditation at all to mindfully concentrate all your attention on the split second in front of you. Just try it.

It is extraordinarily liberating and empowering at the same time to shut out all consideration of everything except the very instant that you are living in now. You are going a long way to experiencing the Oneness of Brahman, the complete perfection of this moment in time. The pandits of India have always told us that Brahman is timeless and perhaps it makes sense that we can only experience Brahman if we shut out the arrow of time from our consciousness.

We are always looking at the clock or thinking about tomorrow so that our conscious awareness is always stretched out and never fully here at the moment. But when you switch off the clock and roll up all your awareness into the instant you will experience that everything seems as it should be and that all is complete.

"This Moment is the screen on which all is projected.
It is always Still and Untouched and is out of time.
There is no difference between this Ultimate
And this Presence"
Papaji

Brahman is like a screen, as Papaji says. It is the mirror of consciousness, the still and all pervading presence of God onto which all is projected. You are part of that screen and once you know this you are aware of your total oneness with God, of your divine nature as part of the One. Strip away your body, your mind with its constant stream of thought and obsession with time and through meditation that is what remains – the infinite Brahman consciousness. This is not an abstraction or a philosophical construct. Brahman can be felt and experienced. Don't be distracted. Be still and experience the instant and witness the enormous sense of empowerment that comes from total focus on the present.

ψ

Explore the connection between imagination and the will. The importance of spiritual imagination is vastly underrated even amongst the religious and this is because we fail to understand the power that can be unleashed when imagination is linked with the will.

"Imagination is the instrument of the ADAPTION OF THE WORD"

Eliphas Levi, Transcendental Magic

The Vedantic teachings tell us that Brahman has brought the world about through the process of Maya, whereby the material reality is a superimposition on the underlying Brahman but has no real existence of its own.

It is as if Brahman has imagined the phenomenal world into existence. Brahman is God's consciousness and through it God wills into existence what it has imagined. But we are part of Brahman too and so what we conceive in our imagination can also be willed into existence by us. The caveat is that we cannot will anything into existence if it is not in accord with God's overall design.

Genuine miracle workers know this principle of imagination and will and those of less orthodox spiritual pathways who we associate with magical practices have also understood it. In the religious sense, however, our object is to appreciate how the religious imagination can deepen our search for the Absolute by bringing the mind more in to tune with our Atman souls.

The Hindu faith is a splendid example of the religious imagination run riot but the power of all the symbolism and allegory that we see, of it as a tool that cuts to the Truth, has been clear to generations of souls. We can also see the religious imagination at work in Christianity where it is obvious to the faithful that for something to be believed does not require it to be historically documented. Cardinal John Henry Newman writing about the Immaculate Conception of the Virgin Mary understood the power of the religious imagination when he said:

"...... there is no burden at all in holding that the Blessed Virgin was conceived without original sin; indeed, it is a simple fact to say, that Catholics have not come to believe it because it is defined [by the Church], but it was defined because they believed it."

JH Newman in Apologia Pro Vita Sua

Just because something is "believed" rather than scientifically "proved" makes it no less true to the believer. And because the believer is Brahman his or her beliefs resonate with conviction and power in the consciousness of God. This does not mean that you can make up any stupid belief and it somehow becomes true. But when the belief is something as beautiful, inspired and soaring with love as the idea of the Immaculate Conception of the Virgin Mary you are then God in the process of becoming. The mistake always is to believe that things are the way they are and that's it. Things are in no particular way at all but are in the process of becoming as defined by conscious will. Things are not what they are but what we make of them. The historical veracity of events in the life of Christ is not so important as what they have come to mean to millions of believers. Pray that one day we will understand the power of our own imagination. Someone that did was the English mystical poet William Blake who knew that when you discover the infinite in everything the power of imagination (which he refers to as "persuasion") is everything. In a mystical conversation with the prophet Isaiah Blake asks:

"does a firm perswasion that a thing is so, make it so?

He replied: All poets believe that it does, & in ages of imagination this firm perswasion removed mountains; but many are not capable of a firm perswasion of any thing."

William Blake, The Marriage of Heaven and Hell

Lao Tzu, the author of the Tao Te Ching, also understood that to know Brahman (Tao) was to understand how we could have power over creation:

Tao is always becoming
what we have need for it to become
If it could not do this
it would not be Tao

Tao Te Ching, verse 41

ψ

Make a picture of God, sink into it, and experience Brahman. No religion has made more pictures of God than Hinduism. In the end it is a very personal thing – these pictures. Whether you worship through Vishnu or Shiva or any from their multitude of derivative deities you are choosing to make reference to the Ultimate in a way that means something to you.

Man cannot describe God so we have to make an allegorical approach but one with real power and lasting appeal. When you consider worship of a Hindu god like, say, Krishna, we have to remind ourselves that this form of spiritual expression has stood the test of some thousands of years and that this fun and colourful deity has steered a vast number of Indian souls along the path to God. What matters is the way you feel inside when you contemplate your God image. Do you feel different? Is your consciousness altering so that you see things differently? Are you experiencing a feeling of inner calm, a stillness and peace? You can't just read about it, you have to try it.

Christians may boast that they worship through an historical figure whereas the Hindu gods have no basis in history at all. This argument supremely misses the religious truth that Christ and Krishna have acted on human souls in equal measure and to make value judgements between our different God images is to tread on very dangerous ground indeed. In the orthodox Christian tradition worship is affected by praying to icons – those magical paintings of Christ, the Virgin or the saints. Is that very different to worshipping the temple image of Krishna? The orthodox say that the icon is like a window into heaven. The Hindus would say that Krishna too is a way of experiencing God – or, at least, an aspect of God. At a qualitative level at least who can really say there is any difference?

The focus of people's spirituality has been so varied down the ages that it seems pointless to try and rank them against each other is some kind of table of veracity. It is not the differences so much as the similarities between the various spiritual paths and their God images which is ultimately so striking. Some peoples have worshipped mountains or rivers, trees or animals. You can approach God through art, see the divine in geometric shapes or mandalas, and experience spiritual flight through music or paintings, the hum of a Tibetan temple bowl or the saying of "AUM". It is the quality of the experience that matters – not how you got there. Because all is Brahman your starting point can be anywhere.

I suspect William Blake was right when he said that all religion begins with poets. It is that sensitised mind which feels

111

into the essence of things and tries to describe that experience by investing places with spirits or gods. It is no less than the soul picking up on the bigger universal soul where it all starts. It is where Brahman has been sensed in the setting of the sun, the whisper of the wind or the play of light on a sylvan river. When these poetical insights become known we get priests and formal religion, said Blake. And it is when religions become separated from the inspiration that gave birth to them that they can go so wrong.

But don't be afraid to make a picture of God. When the spiritual aspirant comes to realise the non-dual reality, that all is Brahman, there will at some point follow an inevitable emptiness and disquiet at the abstraction of it all. Don't worry – come down from your high philosophical flight and start to make pictures. See God as the sacred lotus flower at the centre of Brahman. Out of the dark ground awareness that was in the beginning the lotus flower of consciousness bloomed. The lotus is God, the Isvara at the centre of all time and space who then projects itself as the evolutionary energy of Brahman.

ψ

To know yourself is to know Brahman. To know Brahman is to know yourself. The experience of our underlying reality is the experience of self. When you experience that you are not just flesh and blood and a mind but nothing less than the infinite then you have found your true identity and the circle is complete. You are the god consciousness that allows everything TO BE. The mortal clothes in which you are dressed are nothing more than that – clothes. These clothes can be discarded, as they are upon death, but the body of consciousness never dies and so neither do *you*. But Brahman awareness is possible during life too if only we knew how to open the door.

" If the doors of perception were cleansed every thing would appear to man as it is, infinite."

William Blake, The Marriage of Heaven and Hell

The poets have intuitively glimpsed Brahman and there is no writing better than their subtle verse to express the inexpressible. From Blake to Wordsworth the English poets, in particular, have an excellent metaphysical pedigree and although most were writing long before the profundities of Indian philosophy were introduced to the West they would understand the sentiments of the Upanishads. A humble 17th century English cleric like Thomas Traherne could soar into Brahman space long before his countrymen would become familiar with Indian religion. Traherne may not have spoke about reincarnation but knew that he was somewhere else before he was born.

" Then was my soul my only all to me,
A living endless eye,
Just bounded with the sky,
Whose power, whose act, whose essence was to see.
I was an inward sphere of light,
Or an interminable sphere of sight,
An endless and a living day,
A vital sun that round about did ray
All life and sense,
A naked simple pure intelligence."

Thomas Traherne, The Dobell Poems

In the end we come to an interminable peace and rest when we recognise the embrace of Brahman. There is nothing to describe because Brahman is just I AM. It is the ultimate state of everything, the very ground of being and your own true identity.

The massive breakthrough in human consciousness that is the recognition of Brahman is India's great gift to mankind. It happened in India although it was being glimpsed over the centuries by many other seekers around the world. We have to imagine poetic souls in India of a few thousand years ago who peered into the depths of reality and saw that all was One. They wrote down in verse their inspired intuition that all was consciousness and the material world only an expression, a thought, of that ground awareness that projects from God. And in doing so they found themselves. They found that the truth is not something out there that you have to search for but is implicit in the very instant of their existing.

The truth they sought was staring them in the face all the time. Like those later poets they experienced the ecstasy of Being, the rest and repose of knowing it is One. And they knew that this was no idle realisation, no fancy in some daydream. The greatness of Brahman would draw their breath away. It was like falling into a black void of infinite bliss and for those who could gather themselves in this freefall they realised they had power, they discovered the creative trick of Maya, and they became the miracle workers of legend.

To really want to experience Brahman we need courage. I think that a lot of people who never take on any kind of spiritual quest are actually scared to do so. But even those of us who do explore I suspect only wish to go so far. We know our limitations and worry whether we can mentally cope with what our souls can show us. In a way there is nothing wrong with this because we all have our own path, or dharma, and our own present incarnation may never have intended to take us any further than a poetical, or metaphorical appreciation of truth. Also it is dangerous to utilise the power of Brahman without mental and moral discipline. True miracle workers always act selflessly and never try to put on a show.

Long before I knew it by its Hindu name I myself experienced, almost by accident (it will often happen that way), a brief moment of Brahman realisation. It happened because I had gone not into a state of meditation, but more a state forgetting and loss of ego. My arrow of intention had been correct and in a moment of forgetting Brahman found me. It was like falling into a black void but the feeling was one of the most indescribable perfect bliss. I, too, was frightened. I remember gasping with awe and shaking myself out the experience almost as soon as it had started. Brave are those souls who can not only sustain this state but actually see into the illusion of the world and can access the power of Brahman. Are we meant to use the creative power of Brahman or not? Is this the future of mankind – a superspecies with supernatural powers? We would really have returned home, achieved full self-realisation and our only concern would be what to do next.

I have completed a journey of my own. I have returned to where it all started in Glastonbury to tie up the loose ends and finish my writing. It is a bright spring morning and atop Glastonbury's famous Tor I am sitting facing south east, towards India and where the sun is rising. The hazy light reminds me of Varanasi and this spot, too, has the feeling of a crossing place – a tirtha as they would call it in India where spiritual currents meet and form a kind of an eddy in space and time.

We stop at places like this and for a moment be still. Worldly concerns melt away and we say "I am Brahman." I have come far but not far enough.

Perhaps I have at best sensed the closeness of Brahman but have still to experience the full embrace? How much further there is to travel I know not and nor on this day of the spring equinox when all is hope and expectation does it seem to matter.

The Earth turns, the season changes, but the light of Brahman illuminates all. Know that you are that light and the world is yours.

Shanti

Translations Used

The Bhagavad Gita: Penguin, 1962, translation by Juan Mascaro.

Tao Te Ching: Tarcher Cornerstone Editions, 2008, translation by Jonathan Star

The Tibetan Book of The Dead: Penguin Books, 2005, translation by Gurme Dorje

The Upanishads: Nilgiri Press, 1987, translation by Eknath Easwaran

The Vedas: Phoenix, 2005, Hindu Scriptures, Edited by Dominic Goodall

Poetry of Meister Eckhart: Element, 1991, "Meister Eckhart – Mystic as Theologian by Robert K.C. Forman

BOOKS

O is a symbol of the world, of oneness and unity. In different cultures it also means the "eye," symbolizing knowledge and insight. We aim to publish books that are accessible, constructive and that challenge accepted opinion, both that of academia and the "moral majority."

Our books are available in all good English language bookstores worldwide. If you don't see the book on the shelves ask the bookstore to order it for you, quoting the ISBN number and title. Alternatively you can order online (all major online retail sites carry our titles) or contact the distributor in the relevant country, listed on the copyright page.

See our website **www.o-books.net** for a full list of over 500 titles, growing by 100 a year.

And tune in to myspiritradio.com for our book review radio show, hosted by June-Elleni Laine, where you can listen to the authors discussing their books.

mySpiritRadio